Annette Orchulli

PROTECTED

A Journey of Resilience and Renewal

Copyright © 2023 Annette Orchulli

All rights reserved. No part of this publication may be reproduced, distributed, or transmitted in any form or by any means, including photocopying, recording, or other electronic or mechanical methods, without the prior written permission of the publisher, except in the case of brief quotations embodied in critical reviews and certain other noncommercial uses permitted by copyright law.

Print ISBN: 9798988105548
eBook ISBN: 9798988196555

Published by My Peace of Happy, LLC
www.mypeaceofhappy.com

Printed in the United States of America
For permission requests, email the author with the subject line as "Attention: Permissions Coordinator" to: Jamie@mypeaceofhappy.com

DEDICATION

I dedicate this book to "YOU", my reader! I made it through and so will you.

ACKNOWLEDGMENTS

Thank You, God, for never letting go of me, protecting me, strengthening me, and reminding me year after year to tell my story.

To my children Christopher, Jada, and Josiah you are my world. My love for you all is like no other. You have been my reason to finish this book. Words can't express my gratitude for always loving me even when I wasn't the best version of myself. There is so much more to come for each of you, never be afraid to go after all of your heart's desires. Continue to trust God in every season of your life.

This endeavor would not have gone as smoothly without the mention of:

Taylor, thank you for being the constant reminder in my ear of who God said I am. You mentioned to me that I was placed in Charlotte for you, but little do you know, you too, were placed here for me.

Hannah, thank you for that pivotal push to finally write this book. The night you sat with me to assist me in organizing my thoughts and content was monumental in getting me started.

Jaana, thank you for not just pushing me to tell my story, but for every encouraging word I needed along the way.

Last, but not least, to my parents! I know that I put you through a lot over the years, but I thank you so much for always loving me.

Dad, you would be proud of who I've become.

TABLE OF CONTENTS

Dedication	4
Acknowledgements	5
Introduction	9
Chapter One: *School Girl*	11
Chapter Two: *Toxic*	21
Chapter Three: *Enough Is Enough*	33
Chapter Four: *Party Girl*	37
Chapter Five: *One Foot In One Foot Out*	51
Chapter Six: *Something New*	61
Chapter Seven: *Marriage Unmasked*	71
Chapter Eight: *Caught Up*	89
Chapter Nine: *Red Flags*	99
Chapter Ten: *Identity Theft*	109
Chapter Eleven: *Leap Of Faith*	123
Chapter Twelve: *Figuring Out New*	135
Chapter Thirteen: *Courage*	153
Chapter Fourteen: *Resurface*	173
About the Author	177

INTRODUCTION

I am sitting here staring at this screen trying to get the words out to tell my story. My heart is racing, and I am talking to God asking Him to help me write, to give me the words, to let it flow. I'm like, "Lord, how do I even begin? I did not go to college, and I do not know how to write a book. The most I have written are my notes in church." I am being obedient and trusting Him in this process. People are asking, "Why are you trying to relive this?" Saying, "It is over, and behind you."

I am writing this for you. God told me to write this well over 10 years ago, but I was just so afraid. Afraid of what people would say about me. Afraid of what they would think of me. Was I even smart enough to do it? Would it be good? Would anyone want to read it? I'm like, I don't have the perfect happy ending. In my eyes, I should have it all together, be married, have a big house, and everything else. Fear has literally been stepping on my throat, suffocating the life out of me year after year. So here I am, I'm doing this thing! This time I am trusting God, stepping out on faith, and stepping on fear's throat. I want this to reach whoever it is that needs this. He said this is for you. From the young girl to the grown woman, whoever you are. If you are going through a hard time or have gone through a hard time in the past, and you didn't know how to love yourself more, or choose yourself first. I am telling you that you are beautiful inside and out, and you are enough. Let's take this walk together on this journey.

CHAPTER ONE
SCHOOL GIRL

I grew up in Pennsylvania in a nice neighborhood with my mom and dad, along with three brothers and one sister. It was a small city where everyone knew each other. Being the youngest of five, I'd say I got away with a little more than everyone else. Growing up I remember maybe not having a lot, but having what we needed and trust my parents would never let us know if we didn't have. A time waking up for school with no heat, but my mom had the oven on and water boiling to keep the kitchen warm and breakfast ready. My dad had a grocery store which I worked at different times in my life. I was shy and working with my dad helped to build my confidence by talking to the vendors and customers that would come in. My mom was the school librarian, teacher's assistant, and was also my softball coach. As a family, we would all sit together at the kitchen table for dinner, then we would go into the living room and watch tv together. Holidays were always a big deal. You could always count on a huge meal, enough to feed an army. We always had a fun time with our family.

Every year at Christmas Eve, we always had shrimp scampi, sausage with peppers and onions, Italian bread, salad, cheese, Italian olives and so much more. On Christmas mornings we would get up very early and wake up our parents. We would all sit at the top of the steps waiting for our mom to go down and turn on the tree lights. We would all run down the steps to see a tree full of gifts. Christmas dinner, you better be ready to eat because that spread was bigger than the night before. Family gatherings at the park with cousins, going to cousins houses to hang out and Friday nights out for dinner at Frinzi's, Uncle Wesley's, or the White House Chinese Restaurant.

I grew up going to Catholic School which was very small. We all knew each other, played sports together and hung out together. My mom sent us to Catholic School because our neighbors told her it was the best school. Every Sunday my mom would get us all up and on that church bus for early morning service. Don't start falling asleep. She would quickly give you a pinch to wake you up. Even though I went to Catholic School, I did not really know who God was. I didn't have a relationship with Him, and I definitely did not know how He would be protecting me in my journey of life.

In school back then it was definitely a different time. The nuns would have us line up and one by one we would walk through and get hit with a wooden paddle.

One day, we were in line and it was my turn; I tucked my butt in and ran through so I wouldn't get hit and back in line I had to go. Another time during class, I was tapping my pencil on my desk. The nun got out the holy water and said I was being disruptive. She said that the devil was in me and sprinkled it on me. During school we would have to go to confession. Whew now, this was a scary thing! So, you would go into a dark closet-like room, and there was a screen in front of you. The priest was on the opposite side, and we had to confess our sins. You would sit down and say, "Bless me father for I have sinned." "It has been…", however long it had been since your last confession. As a child, I had no clue what that even meant, so I would just make things up. Things like, I was fighting with my brother or sister. Looking back at it, they taught us we had to speak to a priest on forgiveness and not just going to God. But remember, I still don't even really know God.

In Catholic school I enjoyed playing sports. I played basketball, softball, and cheered. Cheering did not last, but for a year. I did not like how silly the girls were. Basketball and softball were my things, and I was good. Yep, I even got MVP in softball a couple times.

Growing up I used to go to the park around the corner from my house all the time to play basketball. Sometimes, I would go to the college down the street to practice. I lived to play basketball.

I graduated from eighth grade in Catholic school. The next year, for ninth grade, my parents transferred us all to public school. I was so nervous to be in a new school, a big school. I did not know anyone or have any friends. My mom was now a teacher's assistant at my new school. I would go to her class to say hey, and her students would always talk to me. They would always have something funny to say. They made me feel comfortable.

I signed up for basketball and softball at my new school and began meeting new friends. Intramural basketball was a huge thing after school. I would go and play, then stay to watch the boys play. I met a boy who played basketball and we became good friends. And yes, I started to like him. Normally, when the girls team played home, the boys traveled. We did see each other play from time to time, and during our practices. We would talk in school and on the phone.

After the football games on Friday nights, everyone would go to McDonalds to hang out. I would go there to meet up with him. One night he got into a car accident. I had my mom take me to his house right away to see him. My mom came in with me and talked to his parents. I went to his room to see him, and gave him a big hug. I was so happy to see that he was ok. We went out into the living room for a little while with our parents, and just sat and talked.

Monday nights in the summer were a lot of fun. We would all go to the local pool to the dance. It was called the Dip-n-Dance. Everyone would go. We would all be in our cute outfits, walking around, and walking by the pool. The DJ would be playing all the best 80's R&B music. We would dance all night. Who could forget the last dance? It was always a slow song. Everyone would be looking to see who they could get that dance with. Yes, of course, I was looking for him. And yes, of course, I got my dance. He and I talked on and off freshman and sophomore year, but he started dating someone else. We still always kept in touch, and talked on and off.

Walking down the crowded halls going to class, you would see so many people. Everyone was talking, laughing, and just hanging out before and after classes. On the weekends, I loved going to my friend's house to sleep over. We would have so much fun just hanging out, talking, listening to music, and of course, talking about boys.

The days of high school, being a teen, playing sports, and just having fun with my friends were the best, but those times started to change up real fast.

I loved playing basketball and softball so much, and this took up a lot of my time.

I met a new boy. He was quiet and seemed almost shy. He would always smile when we would see each other. We started talking in school, meeting up at each other's lockers, and walking to classes together. We exchanged phone numbers. Back then, we didn't have cell phones, only your house phone. It was definitely a different time trying to get in contact with someone.

As time went on that year, we ended up talking a little more. I remember, I would sneak to get on the phone to talk to him late at night. The phone cord was so long, I would be able to take it up or down the stairs to try and talk. I would go down the steps into the dining room or kitchen. It was a dial phone, and every time you dialed one number it made this loud sound as it rotated back. I'd be peaking around the corner to see if it woke up my mom. Oh, and yes, my mom was on it, and caught me many times. We would be on the phone talking and listening to the *Quiet Storm* on the radio. It was all the slow jams playing.

One night, he invited me to go to his house. We

were sitting in the living room. He was quiet, not a lot of talking, but just sitting and watching tv.

In the beginning, we didn't really see each other all the time, mostly just in school. I remember how we would always meet up in the library with his brother and our friends and just sit and laugh. They would crack jokes back and forth. I was busy with sports as well at this time, so between practices and games there wasn't that much time for anything else. Right before my senior year of basketball, me and some of my basketball teammates had the idea to go egg some girl's house.

So, we all got in the car and drove to her house. It's cold out and dark. We got out of the car and threw the eggs on the front bay window. Running back to the car, we pull off, and we see her brother running towards us, but we drive off. Not soon after, here comes the police pulling us over. The girl's brother got our car description and license plate. We are all scrambling pushing the egg cartons under the seat. Yeah, we are busted. They called our parents. The next morning, we all had to go over to the girl's house and clean that front bay window. Are you kidding me? Embarrassed and mad, we are outside in the freezing cold trying to clean off eggs that froze onto the windows. As we are trying to clean it, who is at the window inside watching us?

Yeah, the girl and her brother. Our basketball coach was there. Our parents were there. It was a mess. My mom did not play. I did not just get punished that I couldn't go anywhere, but she would not let me continue to play basketball for my senior year. My senior year! The one thing I enjoyed the most, over something so dumb I decided to do. She took it from me. She knew that was going to be the one thing that would hit hard and would hurt. I think that was the turning point of me really starting to sneak out to see this guy I was dating.

No fault of my mom because she was just trying to teach me a lesson. I started saying I was going to the park, or going to play ball, and I would go to his house to see him. I would say I was going to see a friend, and, of course, I was going to see him. She started catching on that I was going to his house, and we started arguing a lot. She was not having it, that I was lying a lot, and sneaking to see this boy.

A friend of mine lived in a group home. So, I decided I am going to run away from home, and I can just live in this group home. I can see my boyfriend all the time. Right? So, I did just that. I ran away to the group home. There were a lot of girls there, and we were all talking. The plan was, I would get into the same group home my friend was in. They had to go to my house to see what my living arrangements looked like there, talk to my mom, and ask her questions. Well, that plan did not work out for me. They sent me right back to my house. Me and my mom walked into the house, and my dad was on the couch crying. She said, "Do you see? Do you see what you are doing to your father?" I just stood there looking at him feeling bad. Then, I just went up into my bedroom. Once again, I am punished and not able to see my boyfriend, but I did get to see him in school.

He was starting to flirt with other girls in school and I wanted to say something to them but didn't at first. He would say, "No it's not like that. We are just friends." Little by little, I would see him flirting more and more. Of course, I approached them instead of dealing with him. One time, I went to a girl's classroom yelling to stay away from him. I got pulled into the principal's office. This kind of thing went on a few times with me being in the principal's office.

One night I went to his house, and we were sitting in the living room watching tv. He punched my thigh. I just blew it off and said stop. He punched it again, again, and again. I got up to walk away like, what are you doing? He pulled me back down to sit on the couch and did it again. I remember a couple days later my mom said, "What the heck happened to your leg?" I had a bruise wrapping around my thigh. I told her I fell off the porch. As you can see, things are starting to change up in this relationship.

CHAPTER TWO
TOXIC

Things are changing fast, and instead of me walking away, I am holding on. He is telling me he loves me. So yes, of course, I am believing him. Meanwhile, all the drama in school is still going on. I am in and out of the principal's office talking to him about my boyfriend. Let me just say, he was not even my principal, but he always took the time to really talk to me. He really was the best. Loved that man!

My mom had no clue any of this was even going on. Hitting me is starting to be a thing. He is starting to be verbally abusive as well. He also did not like that I was still friends with my first boyfriend. He was very threatened by that, even though he had a girlfriend. He would talk mess to him being sarcastic about not wanting him to talk to me. He would threaten me not to talk to him, or to look at him. We are going to the store, and my boyfriend is driving. He decides we are going the way that you have to drive past my first boyfriend's house. Now you know I already knew, do not look over towards his house. Don't even peek! We barely get past the house, and he punches me in the face. My head slammed into the window. He screams at me saying, "I see you looking over there for him." I was like, "I did not look over there. What are you talking about?" This kind of thing happened over and over. It was almost like a game for him.

At this point, he is wanting to have sex. I am sixteen, a virgin, and very nervous. I went to his house, and we went upstairs to his room. It was really dark, and we were both so quiet, not knowing what to even say. I literally had no clue what was even going on, since I never did this before. He is saying, "I love you and if you love me, you will do it." I was quiet, and didn't even really know what to say, so I just said, "Ok."

On my way home, he said, "You know your mom is going to know as soon as you walk in the door." Naive as heck I'm like, "What? Really? How?" So, I walked in the door, and my mom and dad were in the living room watching tv. I went straight to the steps walking up them, looking back at my mom wondering if she was going to notice, or say something to me. Now, you already know, she had no clue. That was just a mind game he wanted to play with me.

I am getting caught sneaking out, saying I am going out with friends, but going to see him. My mom is getting to be like, ok this is not good for you to be seeing him all the time, especially lying about it. So, what do I do? I have someone pick me up at school, and I rush home while no one is there, and throw all my stuff in garbage bags. I then went to one of his sister's houses. I was determined to be with him. Well, that did not work out. That same day, my mom and oldest brother came to her house. I went and hid in the closet. My brother dragged me out in front of everyone in the projects. That didn't stop me though. I was still lying and sneaking to see him. Why? Because he said he loved me. It didn't matter that he was hitting me. It didn't matter if he was saying things that were mean, or nasty. He always said he was sorry, and he would never do it again. So, to me things were fine.

It is prom season, and I can't wait to go. Everyone is talking about what they will wear, and how much fun it will be. Everyone is going. I can't wait. I had my mom take me to the mall to look at different dresses. I found the dress I wanted. It was so pretty. It was pale pink. I told my mom, "This is it. That's the one." I said, "Let me check with my boyfriend to see if this color was good for what he was going to wear." I remember calling him and telling him I found the dress I wanted. He said, "We aren't going to the prom." I said, "Yes, we have to go. It is senior prom. I really want to go, and everyone is going. It will be so much fun." He said,

"Nah I'm not taking you". He said, "Actually, I think I am going to take _", and he said the girl's name. My heart fell to the floor. I said, "What do you mean you're going with her? I am your girlfriend". He said, "Why would I take you?" Then, he laughed. This is the kind of head games he would play with me. He didn't go to the prom with me, or anyone else. Again, I was so hurt, but yet, I stayed with him.

Senior year is supposed to be the best year. At our school, we had traditions like, senior week, senior cookout, prom, collecting wood for the biggest bonfire, sleeping out to watch the wood, and then the big Thanksgiving Day football game. I missed it all. Well, all of it except the big Thanksgiving Day game. He would not let me do anything, or go anywhere, except be with him. I was at his house being beat up and talked down to.

It is getting closer to graduation, and I am struggling in my classes. I am not really doing my work because I am so focused on him. Focused on what he is doing and going to see him. I ended up having to go to summer school my senior year, and not being able to walk across the field to get my diploma. I didn't realize how much that would hurt, until that night. I went to graduation and sat in the stands watching everyone else in their red and white cap and gown walk that stage. I got up and left. I couldn't even sit to watch it.

When I got my diploma in the mail, I was so excited! It was in a black and red cloth binder type book that opened up to my diploma inside. I took it to his house. I put it up on a stand in his bedroom. One night we were fighting, which was nothing new, and he picked up and threw it. I went and picked it up and said, "Stop." I put it back on the shelf. He took it back off the shelf and ripped it in half. I started crying, saying, "Why would you do that?" He laughed. He said, "You'll never be anything." The physical abuse was a lot, but there is something about mental abuse. How it can make you feel, and what it can do to you. Yet, I still kept going to see him at his house.

A few months after graduation, I missed my cycle. I'm not sure what to do. I'm 17. I'm afraid to tell my mom, I think that I may be pregnant. I'm more afraid of what she is going to say, or do if I am, because part of me is excited. I finally tell her, and she drives me to Planned Parenthood to get tested. I come out with a grin on my face. I am so excited! The test was positive. I am pregnant. I am having a baby. As I am walking towards the car, she can tell by my face that the test was positive. I get in the car smiling and say, "Yep, I am pregnant."

My parents are not the happiest with me, but they

are still supporting me. My boyfriend is not happy at all, but I am. I am going to have a baby. In my mind, we are going to work everything out. We'll be a happy family.

My pregnancy was filled with a lot of stress and pain. Now that I am pregnant, I am wanting to be with him more and more. We really did not go anywhere together, except to his mom's house. He was still beating me up, and he started to see other females. When I would go to his house, we would argue, fight, and he would hit me. I would always call my best friend to come pick me up, and she always did. I would cry, and she would listen, over, and over, and over again. After she would pick me up, we would normally go to another one of our friends' houses and chill.

I always went back to him though. He would say he was sorry and that he loved me. I would always accept it, and say, "Ok." It was a lot of mental and physical abuse. He would say I was too thin, too fat. No one would ever want me. I would never be anything, and in the same breath, say that he loved me.

At eight months pregnant, he was beating me up badly in his bedroom. I was trying to get away by going down the steps. He just continued to hit me. The phone upstairs was ringing, and I crawled up the steps to answer it. As I got to the top step, he grabbed scissors, and stabbed me in the back of my calf. I grabbed the phone out of breath. It was my mom. She said, "Are you ok?" Out of breath, and crying, I said, "No." She said, "I am on my way". I told him to stop, that my mom was on her way to get me. Turns out, his sister called my mom and said, "If you don't come pick her up fast, we are not going to have a baby." She said, "Brother or not, no one deserves to be beaten, and treated like that."

I went back to my mom's house. My mom and dad were leaving to go on vacation to Florida the next day. I was just sad that my boyfriend had done this to me, and almost sad that I was not with him. I know that sounds absolutely crazy, but this is what abuse will do to a person.

I am now nine months pregnant. I was not seeing him much at all at this time. I am 18, and he is 20. It is time for me to have my son. I had a long labor. My baby is here, 8 lbs. 10 oz., 21 ½ inches long. Yes, he was a big boy. During my delivery, he ripped me. I hemorrhaged and lost so much blood. I could have died. I was so weak from the loss of blood that I passed out when I got up to go to the bathroom. The girl in the room next to me found me lying on the floor and screamed for help. Once they got me back to bed, the doctor came in screaming at the nurse. She said, "She is not allowed to get out of bed. She has lost too much blood."

The night I delivered; his dad came to the hospital. The nurse came in and said, "There is a gentleman here to see you." Into the room he comes. He was drunk and smelled like alcohol. He had a pair of Jordan sneakers for my son. He hugged me, laughing. I told the nurse to get him out of my room. I was so mad he came there drunk. I was more upset that when I gave birth, they realized I had an STD. I remember the nurse telling me, and I was so embarrassed. She told me my son could have been blind coming through the birth canal. Yes, I was pregnant with his child, and he was sleeping with multiple females. I felt like I was going to be able to leave him alone, but I just was not sure.

My first day home from the hospital, I was so tired. My mom said, "Go up in your room. I have him." I was so tired. I would fall asleep feeding him at night. I'm exhausted and trying to figure this thing out.

My boyfriend didn't come that day, or any other day. I really did want him to come see our son, but clearly, it was not a priority for him. His one sister asked me to bring the baby to her house. At this point, I have no car, so it looks like I'm taking the bus. He ended up going to his sister's house and started arguing with me right away. I was backing away, while holding my son. He punched me. I fell back into the tub, all while holding my newborn son. I left and went home. These types of incidents went on, and on, and on.

I was 19 when approved for Section 8. I was finally able to move out of my mom's house. I got a three-bedroom apartment for me, and my son, who is now one year old. It was actually a house, and I had the second floor. I remember being so excited to move in and have my own space. Not realizing it would be a lot to work to take care of a baby and work full time at such a young age. I was still on and off in the abusive relationship. My mom was still helping me with my son though. She would babysit a lot, especially when I wanted to go out. If I would go out and my boyfriend was wherever I went, he would pretty much meet me at the door. He would push me back. He would either tell me to go home or beat me up in front of everyone.

Being on my own was hard, with working, taking care of my son, cooking, and cleaning. I remember, I would cook dinner for me and my boyfriend, and always make more so he would have it to take for his lunch. One Saturday I was home cleaning, and he came with some groceries. He came in and was actually with my first boyfriend. They came in with the bags of groceries and took them into the kitchen. I had just finished cooking dinner and asked if they wanted a plate. I made him his plate and handed it to him. When I was walking away, he screamed at me saying it was the wrong kind of bread. He threw the plate at my head, and it smashed on the wall. He said, "Let's go", and then went into the kitchen and took all the bags of groceries with him. I remember my ex looking back at me like, I am so sorry, and they left.

It became a normal thing for him to beat me up in front of people anywhere A lot of times, it was in the projects. I once was at my friend's house in the projects, it was late, and I heard his car coming around the bend. I ran out the back door, through yards to try and see him. He had a girl in his car. I opened the passenger door. He pulled off with me holding onto it. Another time, I was in the back seat of my friend's boyfriend's car, she was in the front. He reached in the window and punched me in the face. I had a big egg on my head. I was knocked out for a minute. When I sat up, I just started screaming. I was in shock, and I was telling my friend's boyfriend to pull off. The abuse became more frequent, and I started to get tired of it. I put a Protection From Abuse order (PFA) on him so he could not come near me.

One night, I went out to a local club with my best friend. I had a fake ID because I was not twenty-one yet. The music was playing, everyone was out, and it was packed. He had his one sister, who I had been cool with, sneak up and punch me. I never saw her coming. She punched me in the face and busted the bridge of my nose open. People said I was fighting back, but I don't remember at all. I remember a guy I knew having his arms wrapped around me to protect me. I looked for my best friend and found her. She rushed out to get the car. I was walking out the front door of the club and his sister was there waiting for me. I told her, "Look, you see my face. I can't fight. I am literally holding my nose up." I walked outside to my friend's car, and she took me to the emergency room. The doctor came in to check me and said that they called a plastic surgeon in to stitch me up. Because it was my face, they didn't want a visible scar. The surgeon said it was a deep rigid cut. He said she either had a glass or a ring on when she hit me. I went to pick up my son from my mom the next day. She didn't want him to see me like that. I had stitches across my nose, and my eyes were a little bruised. I didn't talk to him for a little bit after that. He eventually convinced me to see him and get back together. Our relationship was very on and off.

    One afternoon, my son and I walked to his apartment. I rang the bell. His roommate looked out the window and said he was not home. His car was in the parking lot, so I knew he was in there. I rang someone else's apartment and they let me in. Once I got inside, I knocked, and his roommate opened the door. I walked in and went right to his bedroom. I saw him in bed with a girl I knew. He and I instantly started arguing. She got up and ran down the hall. I kept arguing with him for a minute, but then I walked down to where she was squatting down hiding. I pulled her out and beat her up. He came down the hall and was now ready to fight me, so I left. At this point, I am so done with it all. The abuse, the cheating, the lies, just all of it.

CHAPTER THREE
ENOUGH IS ENOUGH

Throughout the years, he beat me up more and more. He cheated on me and gave me STDs multiple times. One time, he kicked me so hard in my tailbone I could barely sit or walk. He would spit on me, kick me out of the bed to sleep on the floor with no pillow or blanket. He would tell me I was fat, then would say I'm too thin. He would say I would never be anything, and no one would ever want me. By this time, every bit of confidence had been stripped away from me. The feelings of rejection are overwhelming. I know I need to get out of this relationship, but I don't know how. He is telling me if he can't have me no one can. I am having sex with him, but not even wanting to. I am doing it out of fear. I end up getting pregnant again, and I am afraid. I do not want to have another baby with him. I really don't have anyone to talk to about this.

    I go to planned parenthood to get tested and discuss an abortion. This is not something I really wanted to do, but I knew I just could not bring another child into this world in this broken mess. One of my friends took me to get the abortion. When I woke up in the chair, the nurse told me I just kept crying and asking her if I would ever be able to have children again.

I started to really begin to let go and he could see it. He didn't want me, but he just didn't want anyone else to have me. I decided I was not going to see him and not really talk to him anymore.

One day, I was cleaning my apartment and I heard a knock on my door. I looked through the peephole and saw him. I didn't say anything and crept away from the door. I was trying to be quiet, but he knew I was in there. All of a sudden, I heard the door open. He popped the lock. I was in my living room. I told him he needed to go. He was calm and said, "I just want to talk to you." I did not want to talk. I just really wanted him to leave. I lived on the second floor. I opened the window, climbed out onto the roof, and told him to leave. He said he was going, and I heard the door close.

I stayed scrunched down on the roof holding onto the windowsill, because I wasn't sure if he really left. I was trying to look over the roof but could not see. I started to climb back in the window. I had one foot on the roof and the other on my living room floor. I was pretty much straddling the window. When I leaned into the window to finish climbing in, he punched me in the side of my face and head with his fist and my remote control. I was stunned. I grabbed onto the window so I would not fall out. Once I got myself together, I snapped. I was screaming and charged him. I ran into the kitchen and grabbed a big steak knife. I started to chase him in my living room. He hopped on the couch as I was swinging the knife at him. I ripped my couch trying to get to him. He left. I ran and locked the door. I put a chair under the handle, sat on the floor, and cried. It was like a release, a sense of being free, like he got it, and that I was done. I felt he knew at that point; I did not feel afraid anymore. We were not together, and it was time for me to move on. You can see through this part of my life, I still do not know God, but I can look back now and see His hand was on me. His protection was there, even though it was unrecognizable to me.

REFLECTION

This is not a book to bash anyone. This, unfortunately, is where he was in his life and where I was. Everyone in this book has been through something, and because of that, this may be how we all handled these relationships and situations. As an adult, I have learned that people sometimes do things because this may be all they know. Or, they have gone through something, and this is their way of dealing with it, for whatever reason. Does it make it right? Absolutely not. I am not making excuses at all. I have learned that hurt people really do hurt people. I have learned that words hurt. What you say, and how you say it, will affect who it is directed to. You can see that I have started to feel the rejection, and what that feeling can do to you.

Rejection gives you this almost sick feeling inside your gut. It makes you question how you look, how you feel about yourself, your worth. When someone isn't interested in you, you ask, "What is wrong with me? Am I good enough?" It doesn't matter how young or old you are, rejection affects us all, and can spiral out into so much more. All of this can cause you to feel sad, depressed, and angry. This is why it is so important to have people in your life you can talk to about how you are feeling. Whether it is your family, friends, or a professional. Be open to talk about what you are going through, and how it is making you feel. We didn't talk about a lot of things when I was growing up. As you can see, I kept a lot bottled up inside.

CHAPTER FOUR
PARTY GIRL

After ending my relationship, I wasn't sure how to really feel. Being in an abusive relationship for so long you almost lose yourself, especially being so young. It is just me and my son in my apartment, and I am trying to get back to a normal life. I was still working, and my son was in daycare. My best friend started coming over, and we would hang out, or we would go to one of our other friends' houses. It felt good to not be so stressed out. It was almost like feeling free.

My best friend and I would go shopping in NY. We would go and literally spend every cent that we went with. We would ask each other what change we had to contribute to getting that last outfit. Then, we would either drive home starving, because we spent all of our money, or whatever money we had left, we put together to get a piece of pizza.

My sister lived in NY and worked for Sam & Libby. She told me to come to NYC to work with her and see if I liked it. I left my son with my mom for a week and went to work with my sister in their showroom. That was the best job, and best time ever. I could have continued to work there, but the commute with a small child was just too much.

My best friend and I started going out to the club a lot. Friday night would come, and after work I would take my son to my mom's for the weekend. It would be on! We would drink, and just have a good time at the club, dancing, and just having fun.

On our way to the club, my friend had to go to the bathroom, so I pulled into the cemetery. It was dark, and I really couldn't see. I drove right into a big grass bank. Her ponytail got caught in the visor, and I busted my lip on the steering wheel. When I say we screamed, cracking up, and laughing. I had a fat lip. I asked my friend, "Can you tell?" She said, "No you can't tell. C'mon you will be ok." Off we went to the club.

Going to the club, and hanging out, became a normal weekend thing for us. I mean, I was not allowed to do anything for so long, so I'm enjoying this. We would also go to one of our friend's houses on the weekend. We would just sit outside, and chill. This was such a good time, with no stress, just having a good time. We would meet different guys going out, or just meeting people, and just have fun. It's funny, my best friend would always meet someone, and he would always bring a friend for me. We did this so many times through the years. My friend ended up moving in with me. Even though we did go out on the weekends, I still worked, paid my bills, and handled what I needed to. Remember, I moved out at 19, with a child, so I had no choice. I had to always work and pay bills. It was a lot, but it got done.

While at my friend's house, I noticed her neighbor was having get-togethers on Friday nights. They were having a good time just hanging out, playing music, and drinking. I decided to go over and hang out. We had a good time, and I met some new people.

Now about 22, I was no longer interested in going to the club as much. I'd gone so much when I was really too young to even be in there. I decided, like my friend's neighbor, I would have get-togethers, and house parties. Most of the time, my son would still go to my mom's for the weekend. Sometimes, he would be back in the bedroom, while people were at my house. I would always go downtown to get a new mixtape with all the best old school music on it. I would have my boombox set up with the music playing. We would be smoking weed, drinking, listening to music, laughing, and just having a good time.

Every weekend my apartment was filled with people. Waking up Saturday mornings, the kitchen counters would be filled with empty bottles of alcohol, 40oz beer bottles, and ash trays filled with end pieces from the joints we smoked. Walking through the kitchen to the living room, it would be filled with my friends sleeping on the couch, chair, floor, wherever they could find a space to lay their head. I would go into the kitchen to just start cleaning up. I would wipe down everything to just get ready for another night.

    One Saturday, I went to go buy a bag of weed, so I had it for the weekend. On my way home I was on the highway and got pulled over by the police. I was not even thinking about the weed I just bought. I'm thinking, man not a speeding ticket. He comes to my driver's side to talk and asks for my information. When I went to get it, he saw a baggie of weed. He had me get out of the car to talk to me. He picked up the bag and said, "I'm going to let you go this time, but I need you to dump the bag." I am not even thinking that I could go to jail. I am just focused on the fact that he is making me dump this full baggie of weed. In my head, I am not trying to dump this. I looked back at him, and he said, "Dump it." So, here I am on the side of the highway dumping the bag, watching it blow away. I get in my car and drive back home mad. You would think I would have been thankful that he let me go, and I didn't end up in jail.

During this time, I was going to a local college near where I grew up to hang out. I met some really great guys there, who I became close friends with, and still friends with them now. I would go to parties and just hang out there and have a really good time with them.

One weekend, it was the same people at my apartment hanging out having a good time, when some guys I didn't really hang out with showed up at my house. Everyone was just looking like, ok; it was almost awkward. The reason it was so awkward was, one, it was two completely different types of crowds. We really never hung out with them. And two, they were drug dealers, and just into a lot. As the weeks passed, and the new crowd was coming, the first crew stopped coming. Needless to say, my mom got wind of my house being a party house and popped up one morning. She came into the living room and said, the party was over. "It's time to get out." As people were leaving, she went into my son's room and got him, and walked out. I ran behind her telling her to leave my son home with me. She said, "Hell no! I am taking him." She put him in the back seat and locked the door. I was telling my son to unlock the door, but he didn't. He thought it was a game and was just laughing. I called my mom and told her she cannot just take my son like that. She said, "I can, and I did." She said, "You are not doing right by him." At first, I was just so mad at her, but then I was like, oh wait, I don't have to work and take care of my son. It was like freedom all over again. So, I was good with just going to see him.

As this new change started happening, I started hanging with this new group of guys. I met some new female friends as well. My apartment started getting full of people smoking weed, drinking, and now selling drugs was in the mix.

One of the girls I became close with, we hung out a lot. I would go to her family's house for cookouts, dinners, and laying out at the pool, that was our thing for sure. Come the weekend nights, we would all be back in my apartment partying. The cops started to get called a lot because of loud music, and people are now going in and out of the house a lot, because they are selling. Cars are pulling up with loud music, and more, and more people are coming to hang out. We are all going to this corner bar a lot to hang out, then going back to the house. I start driving guys to do their pickups or drop offs. I remember one time, I was with a friend, and we were at the gas station. When we came out, there were police officers outside. He said, "I need you to drive." I'm like, "I don't know how to drive a stick shift." He said, "It's ok. I will talk you through it." Sure enough, I got on the driver's side and drove out around the corner. Then we switched back.

In the midst of all of this craziness, I decide I am going to start selling drugs. I'm like, I see they are doing it and making money. I am going to make some too. I would get it from them, cut it up, package, and sell it. I would give them what I owed, and keep mine, which ended up not being too much in my pocket.

One night, it was a full house. A couple guys I didn't know came and started arguing with some of the guys that were in my kitchen. One pulled out a gun and shot it in the air. I was screaming, "Get out! Get out of my house before the police come!" I grabbed a kitchen chair and swung it over his back.

Another night, a few of us had gone out to the corner bar, then came back to my apartment to chill. We were in my living room talking, when this one guy came, who didn't normally come over. He was looking funny at one of the other guys. I said to my friend, "This doesn't feel right. I think he is going to do something." She agreed. I said, "How are we going to get him out of here?" We just started acting like we were tired and ready to go to bed. As they were going down my apartment steps to leave, the dude stabbed the guy. Then, they just left. We were so scared. I found out later he had to go to the hospital.

I still was dealing with the same crowd coming over a lot. One night, when I was selling, this random guy came to my apartment door trying to buy some cocaine. He had a stereo system and receiver in his hands, asking would I take it for some drugs. I did not know this guy at all. It scared me. I acted like I didn't know what he was talking about, and told him to leave, and I closed the door. A little later he came back knocking on my door asking again for some cocaine. Again, I said, "I don't know what you are talking about. Now get off my steps and don't come back, or I will call the police." I closed the door and listened as he went down the steps. The one guy that was at my house said, "That is good you did not lead onto anything. He was probably undercover trying to get you to sell to him." You would think that would have shook me up some, but really, it didn't. I was still doing it.

My friend and I were sitting in my living room one night. I was cutting it up and packing it to sell. I heard a knock on my door, so I quickly put the plate and magazine under the wicker chair that I had. It was one of my brothers stopping by. He came in to talk and sat in that chair. I almost died! I'm like, please do not let him move. Thankfully, he didn't. We finished talking, and he left. Then, I finished packaging up the rest of the drugs.

I was at home cleaning, and I got a call from a friend. He said that his car had broken down and asked if I could pick him up. He was about an hour or so away. At first, I really did not want to take the ride, but I felt bad, so I went. I called one of my friends and asked her if she could ride with me. I pulled up to him and he was putting his stuff in my trunk. He then said, "I have some cocaine I need to bring with me." I said, "Absolutely not. I am not putting that in my car." He said, "You have nothing to worry about. It is inside this headlight," which was new and in a box. He said, "We aren't going to get pulled over anyway." Why did I say yes? And guess what, we got pulled over. The officer started searching through my car. The officer separated the three of us and said, "No talking." At this point, I am about to pass out. All I could think about is, I am going to jail. He actually at one point picked up the headlight and put it down. He let us go. That ride home I said, "Oh no, this is not for me."

I'm starting to realize that this lifestyle is not good. I am not comfortable around some of the people that are still coming to my house to hang out, bag up, and smoke. I don't really talk to my other friends much anymore because I had changed. They did not want to be a part of any of it. They were talking about me saying things like, she is not doing good, and is really caught up. I am realizing that these guys are using credit cards to pop the lock of my apartment to get in when I am at work, or just not at home. I tell them that isn't cool and to stop doing that. The one guy had a paper bag. He reached in it and pulled out a gun. He put it on the counter and looked at me and laughed. I was afraid, but I didn't show it. I said, "Knock it off and put it away." They didn't care. They really felt they could just do what they wanted in my home.

One day, I was home by myself and there was a knock on my door. I opened it up and it was a guy friend of mine that used to come and hang out before. He said, "I need to talk to you." I'm like, "Yeah sure ok, come in." He told me that he got wind that my apartment was about to get raided. I said, "Yeah ok. Stop playing." He said, "Nette, I am so serious. Your house is about to be raided. You have to stop now and get your life together. Enough is enough. This is not even you. This is not even who you are." Something in that moment shook me. I felt it, and it scared me. When he left, I went through my whole apartment searching every drop ceiling tile, every cabinet, every corner of the house, making sure there were no guns, or any drugs in the house.

I was actually nervous about cutting people off, and telling them they could not come anymore, but I did it. I told myself it is time for a change. Time for new things and new beginnings. I changed the locks on my door. I changed my phone number and started to look for a new apartment. I found a new place quickly and moved in. I was afraid because now, I am really by myself. I am in a new space, and I really didn't want people to find out where I was moving to, because I needed to make this change. My son's father got in touch with me and said he heard I moved and asked if he could come by. I actually let him. I didn't feel afraid or anything of him. He came by, and we talked in my kitchen, then he left. We actually started talking some for a couple weeks, but I realized quickly, he was the same as before. Nothing had changed. At this point, I am not going back to that type of relationship or behavior. I moved to start new. I wanted to get my son back. I wanted to change. I wanted to do things differently.

REFLECTION

As you can see, I was a mess undone, on a road going nowhere. It all started from my first relationship, which was very abusive. I feel that when there is trauma in your life that you don't deal with, it will affect you in different ways. It also started to affect my self-esteem and how I looked at myself. Thinking, I am not pretty enough. Always thinking, I am overweight. This all stemmed from physical and mental abuse. Even as an adult, you know that it may not be true, but because it was drilled into you over and over, it is in the back of your mind without even thinking about it. It is subconsciously there. The outcome of it is, you will either choose to do things differently, in a good way, make better decisions, or you will go completely left, and your decisions spiral out of control. Initially, yes, I was partying a lot, but it was more just fun having a good time. I had been locked down for so long. My relationship was abusive. I got pregnant at 17.

My boyfriend would not let me go anywhere or do anything. First chance to go, oh I went. I'm looking at it as, I am going to finally be a teenager. I am finally going to have some fun. It was never even a thought that I would get into so much more. There are consequences to every single decision that you make in life. You have to really take a minute to think first, because it will change you and your life. Looking back, I could have been killed. I could have gone to jail. People I was dealing with did many years in prison and some were killed. Choose you first. Do not settle. You are going to be ok. Love yourself and know you are worth so much more.

PARTY GIRL

CHAPTER FIVE
ONE FOOT IN ONE FOOT OUT

It is a slow start to try and start over. I have been living a certain way for a minute now, but I am wanting to make this change. I want to make it happen. The biggest change was cutting off the people that were not healthy, changing my phone number and moving. That was the easiest part. Now comes the lifestyle change. My old friends were talking about what happened to Nette. "She fell off." "She got hooked up with the wrong people." "She is not doing well." The people who I just walked away from are like, "What happened?" My mom is not really trusting that I am ready to change. I am trying to take it from me visiting my son, to have him back home with me. I am in my new apartment. I set up my son's bedroom for him. My mom is letting him come and visit me, so this is a good start to me. I am still smoking weed, but I was not going out. I was not dealing with the crowd that I just left.

I saw my best friend at a football game. We talked and caught up. It was easy for us to jump right back into our friendship, being that we had been through so much. We would hang out at my apartment or our other friends' houses. This new apartment I really did not like, but it was my way out fast. I was there just for a short moment, until I could get into another apartment. My best friend and I would go over to a friend's house. She was the daughter-in-law of the pastor of a local church where we were from. One day, me and my best friend were in their car, and we were all going to a basketball tournament. It was a hot, sunny day, and the windows were open. They had music playing. The music was different, not my normal, R&B or rap, but I liked it. I told them I liked it. I asked if they could make me a tape. Her and her husband both said, "Yes, absolutely."

I asked them who it was on the tape, and they said it was a gospel mix tape. I said, "Oh really, gospel."

We talked a little about the music, and then they started telling me about church. They invited me to come to church one Sunday. In my mind I was like, really church, but I said, "Ok."

Another time being with my best friend and that couple again, we went downtown. Her husband and his brother had a rental shop downtown where you could rent furniture and household items. We went in there and just talked for a little, and again got on the topic of God and church. My friend's husband and his brother were the sons of the pastor of the church they had invited me to. They again asked me to come visit the church. I'm like, I may go check out this church. Everyone I am meeting so far has been nice to me.

I am still working full time now at a nursing home. I am finally able to move from this apartment to my new one. I was just so happy to get out of there. I was on the second floor and had a balcony. It was really bright inside. It was cute and I was happy to be there. My son, who was visiting sometimes, has moved back in with me. I have my new apartment. I have my son, and I am just trying to get myself together.

One of my friends would invite me over to her and her boyfriend's house. We would just hang out. One night, she said come over, her boyfriend has a friend coming and they want me to meet him. I'm all excited and get dressed and go over to their house. We were all sitting on the couches, just talking, laughing, and smoking weed. He was nice. We laughed a lot and had a good time. He and I started to hang out a lot together. He would come to my house, or we would just go out together.

I decided I wanted to go and visit the church I had been asked to visit multiple times. When I pulled up, I got so nervous, but I still went in. It was definitely different from what I remember growing up in. I grew up in a Catholic church, which is very quiet, the preaching quiet, the songs quiet, everything just quiet. This was a small Baptist Church. I was greeted at the door and welcomed in. Music was playing and once everyone was seated, worship began. The choir sang, and then, the word. I saw my friend and her husband after church. I liked it and told them I would be back, and I did. I went back every Sunday, over and over, but I am still half in and half out. I'm wanting to learn and be involved in church, but I am still wanting to hang out, smoke and drink. I am still dating the same guy and having a good time with him. I asked him to go to church with me multiple times, but he didn't want to go. I started to meet people at church. I met the pastor's daughter, and she was so sweet. She and I talked a lot and exchanged phone numbers. I remember one Sunday, the Pastor was doing the altar call and asked if anyone wanted to give their heart to God and wanted a relationship with Him. The stirring feeling, my heart was racing, and I knew it was time. I wanted to go, but was I really ready?

    I don't have it all together yet. I am still doing things out here, but I felt that this was the time. I was sitting with the pastor's daughter, and I looked over at her. She took my hand and walked me up. Tears flowing down my face, I felt so nervous, but yet, so happy. I wanted this to be the first day of a new beginning. I remember telling my boyfriend and I asked him again about going to church with me, but he still didn't want to. He started to cheat on me with someone else, which of course turned into arguments. As time went on, I ended up getting pregnant and he was not happy. He already had a daughter and did not want me to keep the baby. In my mind, I could not get another abortion, I just couldn't and wouldn't do that again. I told him I was keeping the baby. After talking, he said he was just scared. Things then started to get better between us.

    I stopped smoking weed and drinking instantly as soon as I found out that I was pregnant. He went to church with me a couple times during that time, but he was just saying he could not do it. I was three months pregnant, and he said he was leaving town. He said it was too much that I was pregnant. I was shocked and so hurt. It was a hard time being pregnant and just not having him here. I went and talked to his mom just to let her know I was pregnant, and from that day on, she has never stopped supporting me. Our own personal relationship grew just like family. I cannot say enough about his mom and dad, how they have been there and supported my daughter in every way.

    I started to go to church a lot more and wanted to be better. One day, I went for my routine visit to be checked. I was so excited to hear the baby's heartbeat. The nurse came in and started my exam. While we were talking, I could see her face looking concerned and she kept running the doppler machine over my stomach. I asked her if everything was ok and she calmly said, yes, give her one minute, that she would be right back. She came back in the room quickly with the doctor and he started to run the doppler machine as well. I started to get upset. They were both very calm, but said we are not getting a heartbeat and that I needed to go to the hospital right away. My doctor said he would meet me there.

    I got to the hospital, and they rushed me to the room to be checked. They hooked me up to the advanced 3D ultrasound machine. My doctor came in and started talking to me, explaining everything that he was seeing and showing me. He said, you can see that she is breathing, and we could hear her heartbeat, but that it was low. He believed that she had a hole in her heart, but we would be able to see and deal with that once she is born. He advised me that they were going to have to start me on medication to keep the baby's heart rate up and that I would have to go to be monitored 3 days a week. I called my ex-boyfriend to let him know what was going on. I told him that maybe he should come and stay since I was getting closer to delivery.

We are closer to the end of my pregnancy and the medicine is starting to make my heart race. So, I need the medicine to keep the baby's heart rate up, but it is now affecting me. I called my ex again and let him know. I said, "I think you should come now that the doctor said we can pick a date to be induced."

I gave him a couple dates to pick from so he could come. He said, ok, that he will be coming. I also called his mom and let her know everything that was going on and my date to be admitted for induction. I am starting to get very nervous. I am still going to church. I am praying to God about all of this, but yet still being overwhelmed. We are now at my due date and my doctor said he can help some before I get admitted. So, the day before being admitted I went to my doctor's office, and he inserted a Cath balloon inside me to try and induce my labor. I did start to feel contractions, but they were not coming fast at all.

My ex ended up not coming into town, but his mom and aunt did come with me and sat in the room with me for hours, but my labor was so long. I had to get up and walk the halls to try and bring on the contractions more. My friends and my sister came as well and were there with me through it all. Because my contractions were not coming fast at all and dilation not happening, I was in labor for a good 24 hours. I am now dilated, and the time is here. I am exhausted from being in labor for so long. I am numb from the epidural, and I started to cry when the doctor came in. I told him I don't have it in me to even push. He told me everything was going to be ok, and that he would help me. The specialists were there ready to check the baby out to make sure everything was ok, since they felt she had a hole in her heart. My sister was there coaching me to push. I heard my baby cry and I immediately started to cry. My sister said, "You did it! She is here, and she is beautiful."

My friends came into the room from getting their coffee and that quick my baby was here. I am worried and asking if she is ok. "Is everything ok?" They laid her on me and then took her to be examined. My baby is beautiful and there are no issues at all. No breathing issues. No hole in her heart. She is my miracle baby. All I can say is, Thank You God. You are real. You have my full attention.

Her grandmother came and stayed with me when I had her to help me in any way that she could. Her dad and I started to talk some again, long distance of course. When my daughter was 3 months old, I flew with her to visit her dad, who is now in Michigan. We dated on and off for awhile but being long distance, unfortunately, it did not last. But our friendship did, as well as, with his parents. The way they have been there for my daughter is unexplainable. They ended up moving from PA, but when I say they would still do what it took to have a relationship with her. They would drive from Chicago to pick her up and spend time with her and just be very present in her life. This has meant so much to me.

After having my daughter, I felt that I really wanted to do better and be a better mother. I wanted to be an example for her. I continued going to church and started to serve. I am not smoking or drinking, but I do go out from time to time. I am enjoying this time being a new mom. My daughter is a blessing to me. She is my miracle baby from God.

REFLECTION

This was a time of really trying to grow and flourish. I was not just getting to know God, but kind of getting to know myself. I had been lost for such a long time. I wanted to change. It was difficult being new in Christ and not having let go of a lot of things from my old life. I know now that it was all part of God's plan. If you listen to how things happened, He was starting to put people in my path, things happened to get my attention. These things started moving me closer to Him, His protection, His guidance, and His grace.

Looking back, I am still in awe. You have to go through the hard times to come out on the other end. You have to trust Him. He sees you, hears you and knows where you are at all times. It is up to you to tap in. Look for Him in every situation. Let me say this, it is ok to have fun. Just because you are a Christian, it does not mean there is no fun. Sometimes we get so caught up in being a Christian that we think we can't go anywhere or do anything outside of church. It is ok to laugh, hang out and have a good time. It does not mean you have to sit in your house by yourself doing nothing. You have to be smart, intentional, about the people you surround yourself with. It really is ok to have a good time.

CHAPTER SIX
SOMETHING NEW

It is a new season. I am in a new space and feeling good. It can be hard doing it all by yourself, but I am doing it. I have two kids. I am working and trying to do the best for them. I messed up with my son a few years back, so it is important that I grow and do right by them. One of my new friends has a son the same age as my daughter. We have been getting together a lot to do things with the kids. She and I go out together. I am still friends with my best friend. We went to hang out at one of my friend's houses, and I met a guy there. We started to talk, and it just went from there. He was different from the guys I dated before. He had a good job. He owned his own home. He was responsible, and he grew up in a church, where his father was a pastor. In the beginning it was fine. We were getting to know each other.

I would go hang out at his house or he would come to my apartment. He did not want to go to church with me either, which was important to me. He did go a couple times, but that was it. He really did not like to do a lot, but I was able to talk him into doing things. One thing I really enjoy is going to the beach. He would say, no, he really didn't like the beach. Well, I was able to convince him to go to the shore. We went to Florida, and I remember him thanking me for getting him to go. He told me how much he really liked it.

As we continued in our relationship, I started to notice I was not meeting any of his friends. I was never invited to his friend's cookouts or get-togethers. I didn't meet any of his friends, except one, for a very long time. I met him because he was his roommate. Even though he would say he wasn't, I knew he was still mentally connected to his ex-girlfriend. It did not help that his parents really wanted him to be with her, not me. They never gave me a chance. They never even tried to get to know me. Heck, they never even met me, and sat down and tried to have a conversation with me. I met his mom and sisters once, when they came by his house, and I was there. It was extremely uncomfortable because they did not talk to me.

I accidentally met his dad at one of my boyfriend's softball games. He had no clue who I even was, as he watched my daughter and I cheer for him. It wasn't until the end of the game when my boyfriend introduced me and my daughter to him, and it was very awkward. I was not feeling the love. He was not being affectionate. We started to argue a lot, especially when he would start drinking and I didn't like that. I got a new job at an insurance company and met a new friend there. She and I became close and talked a lot about my relationship. I would go to her house as well. My boyfriend and I dated for a good 4 years. He knew my parents. He knew the rest of my family, and my friends. He was good to my kids. My daughter was very close to him. He was a nice guy, but he was not showing me that he loved me. He just could not fully commit. I felt since we were together for 4 years, we should be discussing marriage. When I would bring it up, he would not budge.

I bought my first house. This was huge for me! It was so exciting. He helped me move in with some friends from the church. I had to do a lot of things over in the house. He helped me do a lot of the work. I was so thankful. Even though the relationship part wasn't doing well, he was caring and helped me so much with getting my house ready. I decided I could not continue with the relationship, and I broke up with him. I stopped having sex with him because I was tired of just giving myself to someone that only wanted that. I wanted more. We were grown, and his parents were controlling his decisions. It was a hard time for me with letting go and moving on, but I knew I had to do it. He was kind and helpful, but did not show love, which made me feel rejected in a lot of ways. I wanted to be loved and feel the love.

After I broke up with him, I made the decision I was no longer going to have sex until I got married. I'm sure some people would look at me like, really? You have two kids, by two different men, and now you don't want to have sex? I felt I wanted to do this for myself. I did not want to just give myself away like that anymore. I asked God to heal my heart and help me to do things differently. Of course, it hurt. I had to get through it. Being at church really helped me. I was getting more involved in church. I served in multiple ministries and was meeting new friends there. I began journaling a lot. I was writing out what I was doing, how I was feeling, and just talking to God.

A year later, while at church, I saw a guy I knew from when I worked at the nursing home. After service we caught up and talked while walking to my car. He said he had just started coming back to church. We laughed and talked about some of the fun times we had working together. He reminded me of what he would say when he saw me at work. He would always say, "You're going to be my wife one day". I would always laugh and say, "Yeah ok".

A few days later I was driving home, and I saw

him walking with his two sons. I stopped and we chatted for a few minutes. We realized that we actually lived only a block away from each other. We saw each other at church again, and again. We went on some dates, and eventually, began a relationship. He was so sweet, caring, and good with his sons. He was a great father to his boys. Seeing him with them, how good he was, attracted me to him even more. I was teaching children's church on Sundays and his sons would be in my class, so we started to build a relationship. Often after church, we would go out to eat with all our kids. After eating, we would go to my house to watch a movie.

Our relationship continued to grow. I explained to him early on that I was not going to have sex. I explained everything that I had been through, and where I was in my life at that time. I did not want to do anything until I got married. He said he respected that. Hanging out and getting to know each other seemed natural. Even though we knew of each other quite a while ago, we'd never hung out or anything back then.

Within a year he asked me to marry him, and I quickly said, "Yes!" It really seemed too good to be true. As you already know, I was in a place in my life where I really wanted to get married. When we got engaged his son's mother found out and went to domestic relations right away. It got ugly really fast.

She did not want the boys coming to my house to stay over. All of this had us arguing, but we talked things through.

Before getting married, we started marriage counseling at our church. At first, they put us with a counselor who had never been married. We went to one session with him, then asked to be switched. We both agreed we needed someone who was married. We went to a few sessions and were given homework. My fiancé worked different shifts, alternating days, and evenings. At times, he did not complete the homework. We had a disagreement about it once, but they said it was ok as long as he participated in the sessions. He really didn't like going, but I insisted that we continue because I believed it would be good for us. He started to drift away from going and would say it was because of his job. I was upset, but I didn't let it take over me. We still went to church together and read the bible together which was important to me as well. I was still serving at church, and the kids were getting along well.

One night, he called me late at night to tell me his grandmother had passed. He asked if he could come over to my house. Of course, I told him to come over. It was late and I was in bed, but I got up to let him in. He came upstairs. He started crying. I was trying to comfort him. He started to kiss me, and we ended up having sex. He fell asleep afterwards. When we woke up the next morning, we sat and talked. He was really upset about his grandmother passing. I felt bad for him, but I was so upset that I ended up having sex with him. I really wanted to do things differently this time. I told him even though we did it, I did not want to do it again until we were married. He said he understood.

During this time, I am still working at the insurance company and trying to plan the wedding. I would talk to my friend from work about how I wanted things. She went with me to look at wedding dresses. While I was trying on dresses, I was like, is this really happening? Am I really getting married?

A few weeks passed and one morning when I woke up for work, I just didn't feel well. This repeated morning after morning. I kept waking up feeling sick. I realized I had missed my cycle. Yes, the one thing I did not want to happen before being married, I am pregnant. I was more concerned of what people would say about me, than of me being pregnant. I talked to my pastor and his wife, and we decided to move the wedding date up a little. This way, I would not be so big, because I had already gotten my dress. As it was getting closer to our wedding day, we began arguing. He was now saying he wasn't sure if he wanted to get married. I was so upset! I said, "Are you kidding me?

We are a couple weeks away!" Everything was planned and ready. We received the RSVPs back from guests. My parents and my brother were going to be cooking the food, so that was all ordered. My sister was helping me with the flowers. We talked about it again and he said he was good.

The day before my wedding, my mom called. She told me that my ex-boyfriend, the one I was with before this relationship, dropped off a letter for me at her house. He wrote a letter to me, my daughter, and my mom. I was like OMG, not the day before my wedding! I did read my letter and it was sweet. He apologized. He said he messed up. He thanked me. He told me what a great woman I was, and not to ever change for anyone.

That night was the rehearsal dinner at my mom and dad's house. The next day is the big day! I am so excited and nervous. As I was walking down the aisle, our eyes were fixed on each other. We were smiling. When my dad handed me over to him, he had tears in his eyes. I winked at him, as he held my hands tight. We had a good time at the reception. It was just hectic trying to go around and see everyone and thank everyone. I was only 3 months pregnant, and you could not tell, but my dress was snug. I just wanted to get out of it. I changed as soon as we got home. Then, we were off to the beach for a few days.

I was still having morning sickness. I was waking up suddenly in my sleep feeling like I could not breathe. It happened night after night, and I had my husband take me to the hospital. One time, I drove myself. I had never had anxiety attacks before. I wanted to hurry up and have the baby. I felt very overwhelmed.

My husband worked a lot. I was at home when labor started. I called him and told him I was going into labor, and for him to get to the hospital. I was in the hospital bed, and he was across from me on the couch, sleeping on and off. Our son was finally here, and it was such a relief. The next day my husband and all the kids came to see me at the hospital. My mom was already in the room with me holding the baby. My daughter was so happy to see her baby brother. She wanted to stay with me in the hospital. I went home the next day. My daughter was sick with the flu, so she had to stay in her bedroom. I felt so bad because she wanted to be downstairs with her new brother and the rest of us.

A couple days after having the baby my husband and I were laying on the couch. The baby kept waking up throughout the night to be fed. In the morning, when my husband got up for work, I started crying. I was just so tired. I wanted him to stay and help me, but I understood. His shifts would vary at times, so that made it difficult to have him there. Of course, I have done this twice before, but now I am 35 and it is 8 years later, and here I am again. I am a new wife, a new mom, and a mother figure to his sons. Bringing a blended family together can have issues of its own and we had already experienced some things when we first got engaged. I wanted to be great at all of these things. I was starting to realize; this may be harder than I thought.

CHAPTER SEVEN
MARRIAGE UNMASKED

My marriage started out pretty normal, learning from each other and learning the process of our family. We were going to church together on Sundays, and I was serving as well. I really wanted to be an example, not just my daughter, but for all of the kids. I feel it is so important to have God first in our marriage and our family. If we follow Him, we can't go wrong.

As I said before, my husband worked a lot of hours. Whether or not it was day or evening shift. He worked on the highway, so in the crazy heat he would come home exhausted. Sometimes he'd be dehydrated and throwing up. One time I was so scared. He just laid across our bed and threw up. I ran to get cold wash clothes for his head and neck, and cold water for him to drink. I knew his job was hard and really hated that for him.

Even though he was gone a lot for work, the boys would still come over and stay. We had one of the bedrooms set up for them with bunk beds. I knew it was a transition for them as well, and I really wanted them to be comfortable. I wanted all of the kids to get along. There were definitely times where they would argue, but in time, they started to get along better.

The kids would be so happy when my husband would come home from work. He would eat dinner, shower and then they would all be all over him wanting his attention. Often, he was just exhausted, and would go to bed. When he was working the day shift, he started going to his friend's house, either straight from work, or after he came home to shower. This was one of the biggest arguments that we would have. I would try to explain to him that he is no longer single and shouldn't just be out with them every night like that. You can have friends, no problem, but in my eyes, if you are married, things are different. You have a wife. You have children. I was not saying on a weekend here and there, you couldn't hang out and do things with them, but he was doing this every day after work. I started to realize he was smoking weed when he was with them.

Now this was something he was not doing when we were dating, or I just did not know about it. For me, this was something that I had left in the past and did not want any part of it. I told him that in the very beginning of our relationship. I was like this is way too new in a marriage to be having issues like this. I would try to talk with him, but he didn't like it. I would write in my journal, just talking and praying to God about it. I wanted my marriage to work. I remember someone from church saying the first five years of marriage are the hardest, but once you get past that, you will be ok. I loved my husband so much and I wanted us to be ok. It was very on and off. We would be good and then go back to arguing. I just didn't understand it. My husband still had his house that was down the street from mine, and he really wanted us to move there. He wanted me to sell my home.

    I struggled with that for a little. I thought my house was nicer, and I just felt more comfortable there. I wanted to follow his lead, so we moved into his house. I did not sell my house. I rented it out instead. It was hard to adjust with my kids, but we did it to try to keep the peace. One weekend, the boys came over and my husband said let's watch a movie. We got all the kids in the living room. They took all the cushions and pillows off the furniture and put them on the floor. I got all the snacks out, and we all watched a movie. The kids all fell asleep. We all just had a good time. The times that he would work nights were really hard for me. I would come home from work and take care of the kids. He wouldn't come home until the morning, so we were passing each other. We started having disagreements, and would argue in front of the kids, which was something I did not like at all.

One of the things I was learning about us was, I am a communicator. If we are having an issue, I want to talk about it. He, on the other hand, was not, and would not really respond to me. He would want to just leave the house. He would holler at me a lot when he did decide to talk, and I did not like that at all. It would scare the kids as well. I knew this would not be good for them to watch all the time. I talked to him and said I really felt it was best that we move back into my house. The problem now was we couldn't get the renters out. Thankfully, we were able to get them to move, and we went back into my house. We were still not on the best of terms, but I was still very committed to making it work.

One day, he went and picked up his two sons. They came to the house, and we got into an argument. He instantly started hollering at me. I said, "Let's just go upstairs to talk, so we are not arguing in front of the kids." We went up for a minute, and that quick, he started screaming at me. He went downstairs and told his two sons, "Let's go." I was behind him telling him to stop running and communicate with me. He screamed at me, nose to nose, then picked me up, put his hand over my mouth, and slammed me into the wall. I can see my daughter looking, with her eyes so big. He put me down and left. He didn't come home until really late that night and neither of us had anything to say to each other.

The boys were coming every Wednesday, and every other weekend at first. Then they wanted to come more, which I understood. They wanted to be around their father. I had no problem with this at all. I really didn't. It just became hard because they were with me all the time. As I said, my husband worked a lot, or he would be gone. At times the boys were fine with me, but other times they would not listen. They would say, "You are not our mom, and she said we don't have to listen to you."

Another big argument we would have was about him not giving me money to help with the bills. I would pay all of the bills and it started to become really hard and I was struggling. I ended up asking to see our counselor that we saw when we got married. My husband was not having it all. He did not want to go. He said he did not need anyone telling him what he needed to be doing. We had an argument one night and he was hollering at me again. I called our pastor and his wife. I was crying on the phone, asking them to talk to him for me. I gave him the phone to talk and after some time they were able to calm him down some. This screaming at me and arguing was becoming a daily thing. We would go to church together and act like everything was all good, then go home to the same thing. It was becoming so stressful. I did not want my kids to continue to see this. I would call my counselor a lot, to talk about everything that was going on. It was just too much, but I made the commitment to be married, and I wanted it to work.

I remember one night; he came home from being with his friend and said that he didn't think marriage was really for him. I knew I had to convince him to get into counseling to at least try. After a while, he said he would go. It was really tense sitting in the room because he was just not being open to anything he was saying to him. I started to cry, just saying that I loved him. I said I really wanted it to work, but that we both had to try, or it would never work. He said he loved me and would continue to work on things.

The next Sunday we went to church. I went to the altar to just cry out and leave it with God. My husband came up behind me and knelt down with me. We seemed ok for a good couple of weeks, but it went right back to the same things. I was struggling to pay the bills because he still was not helping me.

Our next counseling session I had to bring it up. I just started sobbing because I felt I was breaking down from trying to handle the household by myself.

I was working full time, taking care of the kids, and paying all of the bills. Our counselor asked him why he wasn't helping me with any of the bills? He replied that he was helping. I looked at him and said, "Really?" I grabbed my purse and pulled out my checkbook register and showed him every payment from the mortgage to the grocery store, and everything in between. I said to our counselor, "Ask him how much is the electric bill. Ask him how much is the water bill. How about a gallon of milk?" I said, "He can't answer. He doesn't know, because he doesn't pay anything". Our counselor asked him why it is so hard for him to just give me the paycheck to pay the bills. He shrugged and said he was not giving me his paycheck. This continued for a while. He was working nights, so often he would not be home for dinner. There were nights I cooked dinner for my kids, and they would say, "Mom what are you going to eat?" I would just say, I'm good or I'm not hungry. You guys eat. I always made sure they were ok and made sure they did not realize what was going on.

    One night, he didn't work the night shift, so he was home with me. We were sleeping and his phone kept ringing over and over. I reached over it to answer it. I said hello and no answer. I said hello again, and they hung up. I called right back, and no one answered. I called back again. It was a female. She started to fumble her words asking for him. I said this is his wife, please do not call my husband's phone again, and she hung up. My heart was racing so fast I just did not know what to do. I just started crying. I woke him up, and of course he denied it. I went to church Sunday morning. During praise and worship, I went to the altar, got on my knees, and cried. I cried to the point of my nose bleeding. A woman from leadership took me to the back room to calm me down and talk to me. We were sitting there talking and one of the first things she said, "Oh, was she black?" I remember being so upset it didn't even hit me, that she really just asked me that. Out of all the things she could ask, she asked that! This is my husband, who I love, and although we are not in a good space, the thought of him with any woman is devastating. We continued to talk. She hugged me and said, "Everything is going to be ok."

My husband and I talked about things, about working it out. We both agreed to work on our marriage. We were growing further apart. He was not coming home or coming in late. At times, during our arguments, he would go to his mother's house to stay. I just did not agree with this. I felt that she should tell him that he was married and to go home to figure it out with me.

I was continuing to talk to my counselor and writing things out in my journal, but it is just really hard. At this time, my daughter is really involved in a lot of things, and I am running her around, dragging my youngest son with me. The one thing she was doing was competing for Miss Pennsylvania. She won the competition! This was so exciting. I was so proud of her. Now that she won Pennsylvania, she was to go to Florida to compete, and have a day in Disney.

My husband said he could not go, so my daughter, my youngest son and I went. The night we got back home, he was not there. I went upstairs and could tell he never stayed there. Everything was still in the same place. I went downstairs and looked on the phone and could see that he used the phone to check his voicemail. I was able to see his password on it. So, I hit redial and checked his voicemail. It was message after message from a female. One was her telling him she was on her way to pick him up from in the back of his mom's house. Come to find out he was cheating again with someone else. He also cheated another time with someone we both knew at his house. I went there and the door was locked. When they finally came to the door, I went upstairs to the bathroom. There was a used condom, and an open massage oil bottle. Again, he denied cheating over and over. I was not doing good, and clearly not able to trust him. He had someone do his taxes and she called to give him some information.

She slipped up telling me about the money he took out, like $15,000, from his 401k. He never told me. When I asked about it, he would not talk about it. He would just say no, and that he does not have that kind of money. He never gave me any of this money to help with bills or anything. I did realize later that this was how he paid for us to go to the beach with all of the kids for the weekend, but that was it.

Things just were not getting any better. He wanted to separate, so he moved in with his mom. I would go to his mom's house to see him. I felt him being there was just not healthy for our relationship, but he really just didn't want any part of me coming there or trying to talk it through. He would not come to see his son or take him. In this time of being separated he was in a relationship with someone else. This went on for a year. It was really hard on me. I loved my husband, and I missed him, but it was even harder for my son.

I would call him from work, but he would not answer. One day, he finally called me back on my work phone, and I was on a call. I put my caller on hold and answered the other line. It was him. I was just so happy to hear his voice, even if it was just for a minute. A couple days later I got called into my boss's office. He said he was so sorry. He knew I was going through a separation, and really struggling financially.

One of the QA people pulled my call and heard I put the broker on hold to speak to my husband. I got fired. I was devastated! Not this now too! I was already struggling with my bills, doing it by myself. I went home and tried to hold it together in front of my kids. I never wanted them to know I was struggling. I instantly started applying for jobs. I knew I did not have time to just sit. Not with the bills coming in. I ended up getting a new job, but it was not paying me what my old job was. I was stressed.

One Sunday, I was sitting in church, and my husband came in and sat down next to me. He was crying saying he wanted to still be with me, and could we work it out. He had talked to one of the married couples that we both knew. They came over with him saying that we should really try again. I was so disgusted I could not even look at him. I said no, and he cried again saying he would be better. I knew that I still loved him, so I said that I would try again, and that he could move back home.

He came back home. It felt so different having him in the bed with me again, I became emotional. A few nights later, we were in bed, and he started to kiss me. Again, I became emotional and just started to cry. I had so many different emotions I was feeling, this is my husband, who I love, but he has been gone for a year. He was in a relationship with another woman. He wasn't seeing our son. He would say he was coming to get him but wouldn't. It was just a lot to take in.

One day, we were talking, and he said I should refinance my house. He said to take some money out to help with bills, we could do the kitchen over, and get some things done in the house. I was not sure what to do but I ended up doing it. We continued trying to work things out, but it just went back to the same things.

Soon enough, that money was gone, and my kitchen was never done. He did completely gut the kitchen, all the way down to the studs so no floor, no walls, no sink, no cabinets. The only thing that was in my kitchen was my refrigerator and a microwave on a step stool. There was dust from the kitchen through the living room from the demolition of it. It was a mess. I told him I wanted a divorce. At first, he did not want to do it. He just got mad. He packed up all of his things and moved out. He said he would come back to finish the kitchen, but never did. I remember trying to figure out how I was going to be able to do my kitchen over. I was already struggling just trying to pay the mortgage and other bills.

My oldest son had moved to NYC, but I still had my two younger kids. I tried to clean up the living and dining room area from the dust and debris from the demolition, but there was so much everywhere. It was hard to get out. The stove was disconnected and in the living room, along with the old counter and other stuff. We pretty much lived upstairs in our bedrooms because it was such a mess downstairs. I would not tell anyone how we were living because of pride and embarrassment. I felt sad and started to feel depressed. Even though I divorced him, it did not mean I did not love him.

Every part of me wanted my marriage to work. I wanted to be a wife. I loved him and my family. I was still struggling with that, along with living in the mess of my home. I would go to work, my daughter would go to school, and my son to daycare. My daughter would get home before me, and I would tell her to just go up in her room. I would pick up my son, then go home to try and figure out what to make for dinner. I could only cook out of the microwave, so what I could make was limited. We would go upstairs to eat. I would wash the dishes in my bathtub. I would order out a lot because it was easier. I pretty much depleted my savings account doing this. I ended up telling my one friend from church, and she would invite us over to their house for dinner and breakfast. I remember the first few times I was so embarrassed and would just eat a little but made sure my kids ate.

In this time frame, my ex-husband never called to check on his son, never thought to come get him, take him to get something to eat or anything. He knew we had no kitchen, and to me, divorced or not, this is still your son. For me it was so important to have an open-door policy, and I told him that from day one. I said, "We do not need to have the courts tell us how you can see your son. You can come by anytime to see him or to take him." The only time he couldn't, would be if we had plans already, of course. Even when we were married, I struggled trying to understand why he would not take our son anywhere or do anything with him. He would take his boys, but never our son. I remember talking about this with my friend. She would always try to give him the benefit of doubt. She would say, maybe because he is a baby. Then it went too well, maybe he is too young for what they are doing. Then one day she just said, "I am so sorry. I really wanted him to step up for him." She finally saw what I had been saying over, and over again. He eventually started a relationship with someone who lived in Florida and moved there for a while.

After a good year of living with no kitchen, I talked to my friend from church, and she convinced me to ask for help. She reminded me how I have been serving at the church and that I tithed. It was so hard for me to ask for help. I had to suck up my pride and just ask. I went to church and after the service I went to my pastor, who is the pastor's son I had met years ago. I just started to cry and asked him if the church could please help me. I explained the situation to him, and I said it is not for me, but for my children. Without hesitation, he said yes that they would absolutely be able to help. We talked about me getting a Home Depot credit card and then the church would pay it off. I applied instantly and was approved. I was able to charge kitchen cabinets, and everything needed to get my kitchen done. Someone else from the church came and put drywall up, put in a tile floor and a new stove. When they were carrying in the stove, my daughter and son were standing on the steps cheering. They were so happy and excited. Like, what kids are so excited for a stove? Mine. Kids who had been without one for a long time. I was so thankful, day by day watching my kitchen be transformed to, not just functional, but beautiful.

  They also took out the old stove, counters and debris that was in my living room. I was able to scrub everything and have our main living space back to normal and livable. It was so hard for me to ask for and accept this help. I had been doing it by myself for so long, it felt almost uncomfortable to have people come in to help me. I also went to domestic relations to get child support, which I already knew was going to be more drama, but I really needed help.

    The first bill came in from Home Depot. I went to the church to show them what was due, and I was given the money to pay it. When the second bill came it was time to pay it off in full and I called the church a couple times letting them know the balance was due, and I didn't want the payment to be late. I was told someone would be reaching out to me. That Sunday in church someone in leadership came up to me about the bill. She asked me questions about it and said it does not look good for a single woman to be asking a married man for help and that I should stop. I stated that I was told it would be paid by the church when it was due. She huffed and mumbled then wrote the check and handed it to me. It was very uncomfortable taking it after what was said, and how it was given to me. My thought was really like how dare you approach me like this. I have been a member here serving and tithing and I was told it would be taken care of with no problems. This put such a bad taste in my mouth and made it uncomfortable for me to keep going. This was not the first time I was made to feel hurt by someone in church. I talked with my friend, and she reminded me, it is not about them, it is about my relationship with God. She told me not to focus on what happened. Although they may be in leadership, they are still people, and can disappoint and hurt you. Remember to keep your relationship with God.

Being divorced is really hard. I knew it would be, but I didn't realize that it would be such a rollercoaster of emotions. Some did not understand why I was struggling so much with it, since I was the one that filed for the divorce. It didn't matter who filed it. It is still a process of healing. It is like death, and you are mourning. Even though it was not good, I never stopped loving my husband. I wanted my marriage to work, but I could not fight for it by myself anymore. My good friend from church knew I was really struggling with it. I was at her house a lot. I was crying, losing weight, and struggling with guilt. The guilt was extremely heavy on me because I felt I made a vow to my husband, but mostly to God, that it was forever. I was still serving in church and doing more in church to keep me occupied. I was doing things to keep me busy and keep my mind off of it. What happened was, I was not dealing with it. I was just going through the motions, sweeping it under the rug, and not healing. So, I started seeing my counselor again to help me through it. It was really hard. There were a lot of tears. I was reading my word, writing in my journal and at times as crazy as this sounds, I was sleeping with my bible. I felt it was a closeness to God and strength. It really was a long process, but in time I started to feel a little better. I decided I was not going to date. I would just focus on me. Focus on healing and getting better. I needed to be good, not just for me, but for my kids.

One night, while I was sleeping God spoke to me, and gave me a word. I remember jumping up and opening my bible. It was Romans 8:1; *"Therefore there is now no condemnation for those who are in Christ Jesus"*. The footnotes at the bottom for this scripture said, *Not guilty, let him go free*. When I say I sat up in my bed so fast, and just started to cry! Thanking Him for speaking to me so clearly. I had held onto this guilt for so long. It was time to let go. It was still hard because I still loved my husband.

I started coaching basketball and would take my son with me. I really enjoyed this a lot. Between serving at church, coaching basketball, and doing different things, I was starting to feel better. It got lonely at times, but I was very determined to stay focused on me and not dating.

CHAPTER EIGHT
CAUGHT UP

It has been two and a half years now, and my ex-husband has been reaching out to me a lot. He was back in town, but still has his girlfriend in Florida. Even when he was there, he was calling me, talking about getting together. He was calling me multiple times a day, then coming around. Talking to him and seeing him again is stirring up feelings. He is telling me he still loves me. He is affectionate, holding my hand, kissing me, and wanting to be around me. The way he would look at me felt like when we first met. Like, you didn't have to say a word, but you felt the love, or was it? We have been through so much, but it felt like we never left. One day, me and my two kids met him and the boys at the park. We played football, laughed, and hung out. When we were done, we went to my house. I cooked dinner, and we all watched a movie.

Everyone seemed so happy. It was a really nice day. My son was so happy to have his daddy there. He was all over him hugging and kissing him. I actually felt bad because he never gets any time with him. I felt like what am I doing? I don't want him to get hurt again. He took his boys home, then came back to sleep over. We talked, laughed, cried, and then were intimate. In my mind, I'm like this is crazy. We have been divorced for a long time. He is in a relationship with someone else, but it feels normal. I am feeling like I want my husband back. I want my family back. I am crying out to God to help me make the right decision, and not be hurt all over again. When he first started to come around, I was like, yeah, no I'm good, but he kept pursuing, flirting, and saying that he loved me. He came with me to our son's games, which our son loved. The norm for him was that he didn't come to get him or go to the games. We went to dinner, hung out, and he came to my house.

Again, we were intimate. I wasn't thinking about my son. Thinking of how this would affect him and hurt him. He was telling me about moving back from Florida and getting back together. So, Sunday I go to church, just me and my kids. My Pastor is preaching, and in his sermon, he is saying, "You cannot go back to who you used to be. No matter what you go through, stay connected. Anytime God is going to shift you, He will test you and see if you are ready for the next level. You must remember what God has already brought you through. There are times God will cut things away from you, cut people off from you. Many times we stay in the past. Let go and trust God has something better for you. People have left you for a reason, God cut them out for your own good. You must do it God's way, not yours. He is not trying to hurt you. God loves you so much. He will cut them off for you. When you let them go, He will bring you joy. Stop letting them drag you around. God has given you the ability to stand. He sometimes has to put you to sleep so He can do His work. He loves you that much. He knows you will kick, squirm, and fight to let go. Know that He loves you and knows who should be in your life." I'm like oh wow God is clearly speaking to me, but I'm like I am good. In that week my ex-husband is still calling me. We are talking and he is saying he wants to get together, and I am definitely considering it. The following Sunday I woke up and opened my bible and as I started to read. I realized again; God is speaking to me. He said to me clearly, "What are you doing? Do you not remember where and what I brought you out of? Why are you going back?" I closed my bible, laid in my bed, and started to cry. I asked God why, then I said I was so sorry.

  Instead of me walking in His word, and what He is speaking to me I ignored Him, and I went to the movies with my ex-husband and all of the kids. After the movies, we all went to lunch, walked around, and ate ice cream. It just felt like it was supposed to be. While we were out, I tried to hold his hand, and this time he didn't. He said we should not act that way in front of the kids. I'm like, huh? We were out other times together, and at home being very affectionate in front of the kids. Now my ego is hurt, and I felt here we go again with his mixed feelings he is showing me, and I am feeling rejected. It was very on and off with him. One minute he loved me and is all over me, and the next the complete opposite.

One day, my son and I went to his house. As soon as we walked in, he started flirting, picked me up, kissed my cheek, and said he loved me. He told me to go upstairs with him for a minute. So, I left our son downstairs with the boys, and we went up. He started to just talk to me, but then that fast he was pushing up, and trying to have sex with me. I told him no. I wasn't doing that anymore and we needed to get past that. He laughed and said, "No c'mon stop playing."

His oldest son came up the stairs, knocked on the door, and said his phone was ringing. He got up and walked out into the hall talking quietly. I left his room, walked out past him, and went down the steps talking to our son. He turned around and looked at me like be quiet, and he walked away. I started to get my stuff together to leave. He hung up and said, "No, don't go. I just had to talk to her for a minute."

He said, "I love you, but I think I am in love with her too."

I said, "What? Yeah, I am definitely not doing this."

In my mind, I'm like how in the world did I get back here in this space. I remember telling my counselor earlier about him and about us seeing each other again. I told him how I was struggling with the back-and-forth game with me. We talked about a scripture Proverbs 26:11, "Like a dog that returns to his vomit, Is a fool who repeats his foolishness."

It warns us about returning to sin. Another scripture my counselor gave me was Matthew 12:43-45. I knew the scripture but reading it again had me shook. It says, "When an evil spirit leaves a person, it goes into the desert, seeking rest but finding none. It says, I will return to the person I came from. So it returns and finds its former home empty, swept and in order. Then the spirit finds seven other spirits more evil than itself and they all enter the person and live there, so that person is worse off than before."

I was like, oh wow! This all makes sense. God has been speaking over and over, and I just keep ignoring Him. I wrote in my journal that I am going to leave him alone. I know it is not going to be easy, but I have to do it. I was writing, telling God to help me let go, to take the hurt away, so I could move forward. Mind you, He has been talking to me, telling me, but I am hard headed and doing things my way instead of His. I'm praying to God to speak to my ex-husband and help him to be a good father to our son. I already know as soon as I step back from him, he is going to step back from our son. This is just unfortunately how it has been. He only saw him when we were doing something together. A week later he went back to Florida to see his girlfriend for a few days. While he is there, I do not hear from him once. No calls to me and no calls to our son. Not even to wish him good luck in his football game. He calls me when he is at the airport on his way back to PA. I was so mad I didn't even answer it. How can I even be mad? I am doing this all to myself.

    God has already told me what to do over and over. I planned for our son to get blessed at church. He is 6 years old now. I have talked about doing it many times, but never did. I told just a few people that were close to me. So, his dad, my daughter, my best friend and her husband, my counselor and of course the pastor and his wife. I remember we were all at the church, except his father. We waited and waited. I texted him. I called, and nothing. He didn't show, and that hurt me deeply. This was something that was extremely important to me. He doesn't show up for a lot of things, or even to come get him, but I thought for sure he would for this.

    A couple weeks later he asked to hang out again. I said we need to have a talk. He came over and I told him that I could no longer do this. This was it for me. We did this long enough, for about 3 or so months. I said no more talking on the phone or hanging out. It was very important to me that we be civil for our son. I asked him to please stay in touch with him. He called me every day that week and then he stopped. At first, I was sad he didn't call, but told myself no, this is best so I can move on. He called the following week and asked if he could come see our son before he went to bed. I said, "Absolutely." That was the one thing I did not mind at all and was always open to. He came and hung out with him for a little. Before leaving, he tried to kiss me and wanted to stay over. I told him no. I knew I had to be strong for myself. He got mad. This same back and forth of him trying went on for another good month, but I stood my ground and would not give in to any of his advances. He was very handsome, so trust me at times it was hard, but I knew he was not good for me. We actually didn't talk or see each other for almost 3 months. Good for me, but not for our son.

Sadly, this is just how it was.

He called and asked if I would like to go out on a date. I was so proud of myself that I said no. In my journal I thanked God for giving me the strength to say no. I wrote I will not go down the same hole. I will take a different route, down a different street. I am waiting on you God. I have been divorced for 3 years now and I have not dated one person, except him. I have been writing in my journal nonstop. I've been just talking to God and telling Him how I am doing and what I am doing.

Work has been crazy busy, along with running my kids everywhere they need to be, but God is keeping me. I can see God using me at my job. My boss would ask me to pray for her a lot. I would share the word with her from Sunday's services and pray for her in her office. It has been a year, and I am doing this thing without talking to or seeing my ex. He was still trying, but it was nothing but the strength that only God can give that I was able to say no, and I am thankful. I was in my own way for too long, and that just messed things up. We prolong God's will every time we pick things back up.

I started getting involved in another ministry at church. I am helping to get the singles ministry up and going, and I am really enjoying that. I am still coaching basketball and just trying to be the best I can be.

CAUGHT UP

CHAPTER NINE
RED FLAGS

Serving on the singles ministry at church is going well. It was mostly women that would come out, but soon enough we had men to come out. We would have different types of events, game night, lunch cruise and get togethers. It was coming together, and everyone seemed to be having a good time. I was busy running my son from sports, to mime, and choir rehearsal. He keeps me very busy.

It has been about a year and a half now, and I met a guy at church. It was actually through the singles group. He was nice. He was more uptight than I was used to, and definitely more quiet. I was like, you know what, I am going to try. It is different, but it is ok.

The first week of talking he had flowers sent to my job, which made my whole day. As we were talking and getting to know each other, I told him some of my story. I told him some things that I had gone through. I was honest and open, letting him know what I was looking for. That I was not going to just have sex with him. Yes, I have 3 children, but I promised myself that

I would be doing it differently. He said he understood, respected that, and had no problem with it. In talking, we both wanted the same things as far as relationship and interested in marriage. We would see each other at church, so he saw my kids with me, but I still did not want him coming to my home. About 4 months in I had him over and he met my kids. My daughter did not like him from the beginning. My son was open to it, and I know mainly because he wanted a male in his life so bad, since his dad was not around often.

    Things were going slow, and that was ok. We went out on a few dates. I went to his house. We took the kids to the zoo, and just talked and hung out. About 8 months in now, and one night I went to his house, and we were watching a movie. A friend of his came by. He let him in and introduced me. He sat on the couch and was like, "What's going on? What are you all up to?" First off, you see it is dark in here, and you see we are watching a movie, but ok. He didn't get up, or act like oh sorry to barge in. It was awkward. The guy I was dating didn't say anything to him, like, we are chillin'. I will see you later, talk to you later, nothing. So, I just looked at him. I got up, put my shoes on, and left. I almost felt like he texted him to come by. Either way, it was uncomfortable, so I left. He walked me to the door. Another time, I was at his house, and it was about midnight. We were watching tv and talking. His doorbell rang and we both just looked at each other because it was so late. He jumped up and went upstairs. He was up there for a few minutes. Whoever is at the door is banging on it. I'm like, ok now this is crazy. This is clearly a female. The person finally leaves, and I'm like, "Yeah, what is going on?" He said, "Oh that was one of my female friends. She was just trying to be funny." You already know, I am like, yeah, not buying it. I said, well, "Why wouldn't you just let her in if she is just a friend? You could introduce me to her." He had a few female friends that he would hang out with, but he never introduced me to them. Red flags are all over the place, and he is insisting it is nothing like that at all. I was mad, so I left and went home. So, now I am questioning if he is being honest in this relationship since there have been a few incidents. He is persistent in saying it is nothing, and he still is wanting to date.

Little by little, he is getting busier and busier with his work. We are seeing each other less and less. We have been dating for a year now, and I still haven't met his friends. He has met my family and friends though. We have told each other we loved each other. Soon enough, he tells me he doesn't want to see me any longer, because we don't see each other enough. I said, "You have to make the time." I asked him if it was because I would not have sex with him. He said, "No. It is just that there is no time to see each other." Once again, here I am hurt. Yeah, I cried, but I'm like, pick yourself up and move forward. My daughter was glad. She said she never liked him anyway. My son was disappointed. He shook his head and asked me why does everyone leave? This broke my heart. This is one of the reasons I don't want to let anyone in. It's hurting him as well. I understand no one can be his father. No one can replace his father. Not having his father there is becoming heavier and heavier on him. He only sees his dad every blue moon. There are no weekend stays, or weekday hangouts. I see what it is doing to my son. He is a very angry kid. He is always taking it out on me because I am the one there, but I do try to talk to him and keep him busy.

At church, it is our Pastor's anniversary. While service was going on, my son asked me for a piece of paper. I gave him the paper. He just started writing to our Pastor and just saying how he loves him. How special he, his wife and daughter are to him. My son loves our pastor so much, and really looks up to him. Every Sunday he would wait, with his little self, after service to talk to him. We could not leave until he did so. After the service, my son wanted to give his letter to the Pastor, but he had already gone into the back. So, we gave it to one of the other pastors. He read it while we were standing there. He asked me if we would be able to stay for the next service, and my son read it to the Pastor and the church. I looked down at my son and said, "What do you think?" He smiled and said, "Yes." So, we stayed. They called my son up to read it. After he read it, our Pastor and his wife got up, walked over to him, and hugged him. Pastor then started to pray for him. While praying, he said how special and called he is. He said, "The oil my father passed onto me, I pass onto you," and he anointed him. This blessed me.

    I have thought about moving out of the area a lot. I initially thought about it a couple years ago, here I am bringing it up again. At times, I want to, and then I get scared. I have lived in Pennsylvania my whole life. I also do not really want to leave my church. Although, there have been some church hurts, I know that they are human and can make mistakes as well. I do love my church; God is definitely there. I just would really like to start over somewhere new. I want my kids to see there is more out there than where we are from. My daughter will be starting college soon and I think a new start would be great. I am really starting to pray to God about such a move because I want to be sure it would be right for my kids.

    My days are full, and I am busy. Being a single

mom can be very heavy and exhausting at times. I go to work, workout, and run my son to sports. I coach basketball. I am involved in a lot of different things at church, but even in all that, I feel lonely. I'm realizing that you can be so busy and involved that you are not dealing with your stuff. You are just going through the motions. I need to take the time to heal. I see my pattern of going from relationship to relationship, and not taking the time to truly heal. I am writing in my journal a lot, talking to God, and leaning on him. I am struggling badly with my bills. I use my credit card to pay bills, buy food and gas, trying to make ends meet. But the bills are always paid one way or another. I refuse to ever be late paying a bill. If there was nothing else left, it was ok, because every bill was paid. It was just tough. I was trying to find another job. My best friend at church has distanced herself from me out of nowhere. I'm not even sure what is going on. We don't sit together in church. We don't hang out anymore, and we don't talk. Just nothing. It hurt, and it was really hard not having her there while I was going through a hard time. We had been through so much together. I had been there for her, and she had been there for me. It was starting to get uncomfortable at church. I actually started to think about finding a new church because of that. We met at church a little before I got married and were so close and always together. It just felt different now. I continued going to church and reminded myself that I was there for God, and with everything I was going through, I needed to be there.

After a good few months, she called me and wanted to talk. At first, I really didn't even want to talk to her. I was hurt and, in my mind, I was done. Yes, I had an attitude. But we met up and talked. She said she was going through some things, and also was convinced that she should not really be having single friends since she was married. It took a minute to get back to normal, but we did it.

I am literally running around like crazy. It is now my daughter's senior year, and we all know that it is a busy and expensive time of year. I will make sure she has the best time, without cutting corners. My son is involved a lot. He is playing basketball, football, in the choir, orators and mime. He said he really does enjoy it all, and I do too but it can be exhausting since I am still coaching basketball regular season and summer league, as well as, serving in multiple ministries at church. I have written in my journal year after year, God I want to move to another area. Where we lived had gotten so bad. There were gangs across the street. Drugs being sold, shootings, even drive-by shootings in the broad daylight with kids walking home from school. The basketball court down the street was filled with people smoking weed, drug transactions on the court while my son was playing. I'm like this is getting out of control. I cannot let my kids think that this is normal. One night, there was a shooting, and it woke my daughter up. She came crawling down the hall to my bedroom. She said, "Mom! Get up! There is a shooting." The police told them to get down. Here we are crawling on our floor to go to another room, I knew I had to get us out of there.

    My son decided to give his life to Christ. He said he wanted to get saved and baptized. And so, he did. I told his dad about it and the date he would be baptized. Needless to say, he never showed up. To me, this was just not ok. This was a huge day for our son. But it is ok, I have told him over and over about the importance of being there for our son. I remember telling him that God will not allow his life to be right until he gets right with our son. Many times, my son would ask where his dad was or is his dad coming, and I didn't bash him. I would say he was busy, or he was at work. I remember one year on my son's birthday; I gave him his favorite gift that he wanted. I said it was from his dad, so he would have something from him. Heck, the majority of the time, I would have to take him to the barber shop. No woman wants to sit up in there with all those men talking crap.

    About a year later, my son started having severe anxiety attacks. The first one actually happened at the barber shop. I was friends with the barber, and on this day, I was home cleaning, and asked him to call me when he was done cutting my son's hair. I would come get him. He called early and said, "I think you need to come get him." I was like, "What is wrong, everything ok?" He said, "I don't know." He said my son said he felt like he couldn't breathe and was having a heart attack. I flew out the door to go get him. Thankfully, we lived close. I was nervous because I remember his dad telling me he had a heart attack at like 8 or 10 years old. I got my son and just started asking him about how he was feeling, and what symptoms he was having. After talking with him, I really felt like he had an anxiety attack, but he was so worked up I took him to the emergency room to be safe. I called his dad to tell him. He met us at my house. They ran some tests on him and said he was ok. His heart looked fine, and they believed it was an anxiety attack as well. He was still so worked up, so I made an appointment with his doctor and then was referred to a pediatric heart specialist. His dad and I went to the specialist appointment with him. They told him he has a very healthy heart. He had so many questions, and the doctor kept emphasizing to him that all the tests were clear. Even with all of this and all the tests done, my son was still so worried.

His anxiety attacks continued over and over. It would wake him up from his sleep and he would come down the hall to my room. We would pray and he would go back to bed. Some nights he would just sleep in my room. In time, I got him into counseling for his anger and anxiety both. He really didn't want to talk to them. I took him to two different counselors. The one was a guy and after a couple sessions he asked for his dad to come into one of the sessions. He did come to the one session. Then, I took him to a woman. He opened up a little more to her, but he just really did not want to talk. This process was a lot. He was up almost every night, and I had to be to work by 5am, so I was exhausted mentally and physically. He continued to play basketball and was still involved in church. I asked the youth pastor to talk and spend time with him, and he did.

CHAPTER TEN
IDENTITY THEFT

I got my son hooked up with a basketball trainer to do one-on-one training. Keeping him active was important for his mental and physical health. He was on different basketball teams, so I needed him to get polished. One of my friends told me she knows a guy who trains, and that he is really good. She said he trained her son as well, and that he played some professional ball, so he knew what he was doing. I knew it was going to be expensive, but I really wanted to get him right for the school and the traveling teams. I called and set it up. He said he has a set up in his yard at his house where he would train him. My son was so excited to have this one-on-one training.

First session I went, met him, and talked for a few minutes on what he would be doing, then left. The first few times I would just drop him off and leave. One day, he told me I could stay, hang out and watch. I was like, "Oh ok sure." I sat on the wall watching. It was summer and man it was so hot out. But I didn't mind because I liked seeing what he was doing with my son. Remember, I played basketball and still coach, so I enjoy this. The coaching side of me kept wanting to say something while my son was training, and he knows me, so he would look over at me like, mom, don't you dare. A few weeks into training, I got a text from my son's trainer asking me how I was doing and what I was up to. We texted a little and then said, "Ok, see you at the next training session." I guess you can see where this is going. He is starting to pursue me and I'm like, yeah, no I can't do this. Yes, it has been a couple years since my last relationship, but I am still working on trying to be the best me. At this time in my life, I am full, doing good emotionally and mentally. My relationship with God is good. I am very involved in serving in many ministries at church, and my son is involved as well. Am I lonely for companionship? Yeah, I am, but I am trying to stay focused.

There is an evening summer league in the area where I live that I always go to. Where there is basketball, I am normally there because either my son is playing, I am coaching, or I am watching. I love it. One night, he texted me and asked me to come and watch him play. So, I went and watched. Where I am from, we all know each other, especially with all the sport events we go to. So, I was up there watching the games and just talking to people. After his game, I was still hanging out, and then I left. I was walking away from the court and down towards the parking lot, and he was calling my name, and running towards me. I stopped and turned around and he was like, "Where are you going?" We stood there talking for a while, and everyone was starting to leave. He came there with his friend, who was leaving. He asked me if I could take him home, so we could stay and talk. I said, "Yeah sure." So, he told his friend to go, and we stood out there talking for a while. We got in my car to sit and talk some more. On the way to his house, he asked me if I would just drop him off at his sister's house. So, I pulled up to his sister's house and we sat out front of her house for a little, then I left.

    The training continued, and so did us talking getting to know each other. He invited me over to his sister's house one night and I met her, her husband, and the kids. Everyone was really nice and down to earth. I am going with him to his sisters a lot. We would sit up watching tv, talking, and soon enough he kissed me. He starts coming to my house at night, when my kids are sleeping, and then I take him to his sister's early in the morning. I am trying not to let them see him, because I have not had any men sleeping over since my ex-husband. I am definitely curious though, why are we not ever going to his house? We went to his house one night and sat outside talking. We ended up going inside. He was kissing me, and the chase was on. I said, "No," but it was hot and heavy.

It was dark though. So, I finally asked him, and he said there were some things going on with his house. He is not living there right now, and has the power cut off. He then tells me that he is married, but they have been living separately for 2 years. He said she lives with their kids, and she has a boyfriend. Ok, so now I'm like wait, what! He continues to tell me there is nothing to worry about, that they co-parent, and that is all. He said they have discussed divorce before. We had been seeing each other for 3 months, like you should have told me something. When I would take my son to his house for training it was daylight, so he didn't need the lights on, so I wasn't thinking about that. His truck was in the shop, so he had his friends, family, and me to get him around. Instead of me paying attention to all of this, I believed him and swept it under the rug and kept seeing him, ignoring the flags, again.

He ended up moving in with me, which is something else I said I would not do. I have protected my kids as far as having men in my home or sleeping over. It was just something I did not do. But........., I did this time. And after 6 or so years of not being intimate with anyone but my ex-husband, I decided to be intimate with him. Something about that made me so emotional and I cried. Of course, I wanted to, but I had made that promise to myself that I was not going to do things the same way. I was not going to give myself to anyone until I got married again. He was still training my son, and he also coached at a local community center. He was definitely busy. I was cooking him dinner every night and packing his lunch. He would go back to his hometown to go out here and there, but I did not go with him. We would do things locally or go to his sister's house. I met his mom, who was so sweet. I got along well with her and his sister.

    I would always ask him to go to church with me, but he would either train someone or play on this recreation flag football team. I started to change. I started to drink more. I wanted to go out, and the worst thing that I could do was stop going to church, and I did. I would still take my son to church for choir, play and mime rehearsals, but I would not go in. I would drop him off and go back to pick him up. I was off and on, going to service on Sunday, and at times, I would just drop my son off. My best friend stopped talking to me again. She was not happy with the changes I had made, and she was going through some things of her own. I have been going to my church for a good 19 years now and have served in almost every ministry.

No one had reached out to me once to see if I was ok. Although I knew they were busy with other church members it still hurt.

At one point, two of my friends knew something was going on and messaged me that they missed seeing me at church, and wanted to get together, if I wanted to. This meant a lot, but I did not meet up. My daughter was home for the summer from college, and she said to me, "Eeeewww mom, I don't even know who you are right now."

And I told her. "I have been an example for you for a long time, but this time don't follow my lead."

I was changing, allowing things I should not have, and knowing I deserved better. He said he was going through a lot with his house, his truck that broke down, and he was mentally very stressed. I would pray for him, encourage him, and just try to help how I could. I let him use my car. So, we would get up early, he would drop me off to work, because I had to be to work by 5am. He would go back to the house to get ready for work and use my car. I got done from work before him, so I would walk home from work. My neighbor saw me walking home after work one day. He said, "Miss, are you ok?"

I said, "Yeah, I'm good."

He said, "Miss, don't let him do you like that.

You should not be walking home."

He said, "He is a grown man, and if anyone should be walking it should be him."

I laughed and said, "It's ok. I am good. My job is not far from here."

He was pretty much doing his thing, and just living with me for free. He gave me $100 twice in that year and a half time frame. I would talk to him a lot about opening his own space to train and start AAU teams. I knew this would be really good for him. I was trying to help him in any way that I could. He ended up getting an assistant coaching job at one of the high schools. I was so happy for him.

He worked hard for this position. I would go to his games, but he would act differently, like he wasn't with me. He got his truck back and I had this feeling when he did that, things were going to start to change, and they did. He was gone a lot. He would come in late or not come at all. Christmas eve he never came home that night, so Christmas day I was no good. I was crying and trying to be ok for my kids, but I was just messed up. We had been together for a year now, and things had only gotten worse. I found out that he had met up with someone at a hotel. He said they were friends for years. Then he was on the phone with her a lot. I said, "If she is just a friend, you can tell her you are in a relationship, and cannot talk like that."

I said, "As a friend she would understand that."

We continued to argue about that, along with other things. He called me, said he was sorry, and that he wanted to be with me. The next day he kept texting me that he was so sorry and that we would be ok. Once again, I believed him. Things only got worse, and I knew I could not do it anymore. He moved out and went back to his sister's house. I was so hurt, and so was my son. He was so sad once again because he wanted a male figure so badly. I could not get out of my bed, and I struggled with going to work. His mom would call and check on me. She knew I was hurt. I called my best friend, and even though things had not been good, she came right over. I was in my bed, and she came over and sat on my bed as I cried.

For whatever reason, this one really messed me up. I knew better, but because I was lonely, because he pursued me, and told me what I wanted to hear, I accepted it all. After all those years of broken relationships, although I was lonely for companionship, I was really in a great place. I was still struggling financially, but I was in a good head space. When we met, I was so involved in my church. I was serving in many ministries. My son was very involved in church and sports. I had so much joy. When we met, he was not in a good place. He was going through a lot of things. He was hurting and empty. I felt like I almost nurtured him, prayed for him, and helped him. By the end of our relationship, it flipped. I felt like he had sucked all the life out of me. He was full, thriving at his new job, had his truck back and was doing his thing. Now, I was empty. I wrote it all in my journal. I cried and cried out to God day after day to please help me. I wrote in my journal talking to God. I said, "I am so sorry for all of my mess."

  I asked for forgiveness and asked Him to please help me to get through this hard time. I am trying so hard to get back to me and to be close to Him. I continued to write that I am going through a lot. My heart is broken. I am mending a broken friendship. I am trying to get back to praying, talking to God, and going back to church. I am writing in my journal not missing a day talking to God to help me pretty much get over him and the pain to go away. I would have worship music playing nonstop in my bedroom. I would also go for a lot of walks to think. Going downtown to sit by the water and write in my journal was something I was doing a lot. His mom and sister had called to check on me, and both are apologizing for how he didn't do right by me. His mom said he was selfish and was only thinking of himself. She was so sweet. She would always end our conversations saying she will pray for my healing, and saying, "Never say goodbye. We say see you later."

A month has passed, and it is my birthday. A bunch of friends took me out to eat after church. We had such a good time talking, laughing, and sharing stories. A few of us were going through some of the same things. It was a very much needed time, and I was thankful. This time of healing for me took much longer than I would have wanted. I really struggled with moving past this hurt. Journaling, along with writing poetry, was helping to release.

As time passed, my son is still really going through. He is so angry and taking it out on me. I know it is because his dad is not in his life and since I am the one with him, I get the hit of it. I am trying to be understanding and loving about it, but it can be hard. We have been through this over, and over again.

It has been five months since we broke up. It is harder some days than others. I was going to work one morning, my street is a one-way street, so I was going up and two blocks up. Who do I see? My ex! I see him coming out of a house getting into his truck. I was so shocked at first like what the heck is he doing over here. Come to find out, he is dating someone and living there. I said, "Really? On the same street two blocks up." I had to drive that way to work every day, so I would see him. So, I started to take a different route.

I spoke to my daughter's grandparents, and we planned to go and see them in Chapel Hill, NC. We drove and spent a long weekend with them. It was so nice to get away. It was beautiful there. We just hung out and enjoyed our time together. While there, I brought up again how I have been really wanting to move, relocate. Her grandmother said you should move to Charlotte. It is up and coming and a great place for the kids to grow. It was definitely something to think about. My son is still struggling with his anxiety, and at times, it is really a lot. I have prayed for him, over him, over our house. He has been to counselors. I talked to two different men at church that I was friends with. They both, at different times, took the time to speak to him, to try and help him. I got a call from my son while I was at work. He had an anxiety attack in school and was in the office. When we are not together and it happens, he will call me, and I am able to talk him down. When I got home from work that night, I got out my bible and was just showing him scriptures and talking to him. I had printed some scriptures out at work and together we made a collage for him to have in his room, to carry in his backpack, if he needed it, to have as a reminder. We talked about our testimony, tests, and trials. What we go through, and how we will be able to help someone else. What he is going through, he will be able to help someone experiencing the same thing. I said, "I am going to write my book about my life, and how hopefully it will help someone."

He said, "Really?"

I said, "Yeah, I'm doing it."

He said, "It will be in Barnes and Noble!"

I said, "Ok you better speak it to be there."

I am afraid to write, and don't know how, but I know God has told me over and over, year after year. I prayed for Him to help me, to open doors for my book and to give me the confidence to write. I have to start it.

The process is hard, and none of us really want to go through it. We are afraid and scared. We all want it fixed now, quick, and fast. But no, you must go through. The word *through*, says it clearly. It means you will come through. It means you will come out the other end. You must trust God when you are in it. You must believe Him. You will feel it. God will remove things and it will hurt, but it won't break you. He will reshape you, prepare you, build you up and get you ready to go through. I am trusting Him through this process.

I was cleaning my house and I had to run my son to his friend's and my daughter to work. I was in and out of the house a few times just rushing around.

I came home and sat on my couch for a minute and all of a sudden, I felt such a calmness come over me. A reassurance that I would be ok. In the midst of our busy lives, it is easy to get overwhelmed, but feeling God's presence was something I needed in that moment. He reminded me that He is right here. He is protecting me, and I am thankful.

IDENTITY THEFT

CHAPTER ELEVEN
LEAP OF FAITH

It has been about a good year and a half since my breakup. I am doing good and really trying to work on me. My son still has me very busy with all of his activities. Sadly, he is still really struggling with his anxiety. He will be starting high school next year and I just want him to be good all the way around. He is still playing basketball at school and miming at church. I have reached out many times to the pastor and youth pastor to see if they were available to talk to him. Get him hooked up with someone to really talk to him and help me. I am a single mom with a teenage son. Raising a son by yourself is just not easy. As a woman I can't teach him how to be a man. I can only teach him so much and he will only tell me so much.

What I do know, is that he is angry, he has anxiety, and he is struggling with a lot of different emotions. I was pretty much crying out for help, and I feel they dropped the ball and did not follow through. Church hurt is not easy to deal with, especially when it has happened multiple times. I have been attending this church for twenty-three years. I have served and my children have been very involved as well, so it made it very hard. I know their plates are full as well, I just wanted some direction, some help for him. I started talking to my kids again about moving. I was praying more about this move. I felt it in my soul it was time to go, that God was saying this is it.

    The time is now. One night, I asked the kids how they would feel about moving to Charlotte, NC and starting over new. My daughter was a Junior in college and my son was in eighth grade. They both said, yes right away and were very excited about it. I told them if we do move that it would be fast because I wanted to be in Charlotte the summer before my son would start High School so it would give him at least a good month to possibly meet some friends before starting school. I called a friend who is a realtor and we talked about what I needed to do to get my house ready. My ex from years ago came and he helped me so much. I was so thankful. He cleaned out the basement, did some touch ups on the deck, and a few repairs in the house. I went through the house and started to get rid of things we didn't need.

    I sold some big items and just got things ready. My realtor had her stager come over and she rearranged a few things and added some things. She was great. My house is ready and on the market. I was so nervous because remember we do not live in the best neighborhood. I prayed and prayed and asked God please do not let there be any drug raids, no shootings, no noise, no nothing. I said, "God, if it is Your will that we make this move to NC, then my house will sell, and it will be an easy transition."

Let me tell you how my God did just that! We got offers on the first day, second day and third day on the market. My house sold in three days, and it was a cash offer. I knew it. I felt that it was going to sell fast. God was doing it and doing it quickly. My plan was if I sold my house we would put our things in storage for 30 days, stay with my friend, and then the next month be on the road to Charlotte. To be nice, and as a courtesy, I called my son's father and told him that we were going to be moving out of the area. He was not happy at all, he started to holler at me calling me a F….. B and how dare I take his son away. I said, "You have not been there for him in how long, but I felt out of respect I would call and tell you."

We went back and forth arguing and then he said to tell my son to call him when he gets home. When my son got home, I told him his dad wanted him to call him. So, he called his dad and while on the phone with him I can see his face and he's upset. He was trying to explain to his dad that this was going to be good for him. That it would be a fresh and new start, new beginning and he was excited. His father started to holler at him, and he hung up on my son. My son stood there with his eyes so big and his face blank. I thought something happened, I said, "What? What is wrong? Are you ok?"

He started to cry, and he said his dad told him he never wanted to see him again. I grabbed him and hugged him and said, "It is ok, you're ok. Your dad is just upset. He will be ok."

After my son went to bed, I tried to call his dad back to be like how dare you say that to your son, but he did not answer. I was shocked that he would say something like that to his son. I thought his dad would cool off and call my son or see him, but he didn't.

My daughter was on summer break from college, so she and I went to Charlotte twice to look at apartments. I wasn't sure where to go or where to look. I contacted her one cousin, and she gave me an area to start looking. The first time my daughter and I went we didn't really come up with anything. The second trip me, my daughter and my son went. It was so hard because we were only there for the weekend each time because we had to get right back so I could work. Places were closing and they did not want to take the time to show us. Then the last place we looked at the woman was so nice. She was closing as well but said, "It's ok. I can take the time to show you around."

Well, that was all she wrote. We went back the next morning and signed the lease. We went back home, we packed everything up and put it all in storage, then we went and stayed at my friend's house. Yep, for thirty days. I had applied to so many jobs but was just not getting any calls. The closer it got to the 30 day mark I was getting a little nervous and my friend was like, "Nette, I don't think you should go yet, give it a little more time."

I said, "No, we have to go. I have a plan and I am going to stick to it."

It was getting closer to saying goodbye to everyone, and I knew it would be hard. I think one of the most emotional moments was leaving our church. That is where I started my Christian walk. That is where I met God, and where I grew in Him. I learned a lot, met a lot of good people and friends. My children grew up there and had also met some friends. We also had some disappointments and hurts there. Our last Sunday there, my son mimed one last time and when he was finished, he just leaned over and cried, it was a lot of mixed emotions. We also decided as a family to all get baptized again that same Sunday, to leave every hurt in the water and be ready to start new. Thirty days came and we packed up the rental truck and off we drove early that morning. I drove the truck and my daughter drove my car behind me. My son rode with her the longest, and then he got in the truck with me. I hired movers in Charlotte to meet us at our new apartment so they could unload for us. We really did it. We moved to a whole other state. Left all of our family and friends behind and started new. I had no job, no nothing. I had lived in Pennsylvania my whole life and never really thought I could do something like this. But guess what, we did. God had a whole other plan.

We are all set up in our new apartment, the kids picked their room and are both happy. We are excited about getting out and exploring everything. My daughter's grandparents came over and hung out with us and helped us get some things set up and put together. When we all woke up the next morning we said the same thing, it was so quiet. We are used to people outside loudly, cars, music, fights. It was completely quiet and that was good. We had a pool in our complex so the first morning we went outside and sat at the pool for a little. My daughter was only here for a month because she had to go back to PA to finish out college. It was her senior year. While she was here though, we explored our new city. We saw that we lived by the outlets, so we went and did some shopping for school. The first Sunday we went to church, we went to Elevation Church in Ballantyne which was a completely different experience for all of us. It was very different from what we were used to, but we were open to this new experience. We heard them talk about Love Week when we were at church, so we jumped in and served at a school, painting murals on the walls. We really had a good time. I did not have a job, so a lot of my time was looking for a job. I didn't think it would be so hard since I had so many years of healthcare experience. I was applying nonstop and getting no calls.

I had the money from the sale of my house, but it was not a lot, so I knew I needed to move on this fast. We have been here a little over a month and one day we were at TJ Maxx shopping. I saw they had a hiring sign up. I was like, well, I need some kind of income so I guess I will apply. I filled out the application and took it in. They interviewed me on the spot and hired me. I went out to my car and my daughter was waiting for me. She said, "Well, how'd it go?" I told her they hired me. She said, "Oh mom that is great, good job."

I started to cry. She said, "Wait. What is wrong."

I told her I am thankful for the job because I do need some kind of income right now. I have so much experience. I will be working for $9.00 an hour, which I haven't worked for that little in many years. But I knew I needed it, so I had to be thankful. I was praying and telling God, "You brought me down here and I need a job. I know You did not bring me this far to just have nothing for me."

A couple weeks later I got a call for an interview at a doctor's office not far from where I lived. I went to the office, and it was the two doctors that did the interviewing. We talked at length, and they were very impressed by my resume. They told me it was a brand-new office about to open and they felt that I could be perfect for the financial counselor position. They explained it was not routine medical, it was stem cell therapy, so it was a trial run for this office location. They had other offices further down in SC. I kept my job at TJ Maxx to be safe. I was new to the area and needed a job, so I jumped right in. I started right up the following week. It was a small staff, but I was open to learning something new and to just be working.

How great it was that we were all Christians working in this doctor's office. We prayed every morning before opening the door. This really blessed me. I worked there for four months. One night, I was leaving out and the one doctor called me into his office. He said that they were eliminating my position because they were not growing there fast enough. I was so shocked and upset. I left and got in my car and just cried. Like, what! I just started here. I just moved here. This cannot be happening. Again, I'm like, God what is going on? I clearly heard you say for us to move here. I picked up more hours at TJ Maxx and I continued applying to many jobs.

I had one interview at a hospital, but they emailed me and said they went with someone else.

It is my birthday weekend and three of my friends came from home to celebrate my 50th birthday. We had such a great time hanging out and celebrating. It was just so good to see them. I had only been down here a few months, so to have friends come see me was amazing. It was so good to see them. One month later, another visitor! I am so happy my friend and her daughter came to see me. We spent Thanksgiving together and had a great time. Having my friends visit meant so much to me. I'm telling you, moving far away with no one, you need your people.

Four months from the time I got fired, I got a call from a family practice in SC. The office manager and front desk lead interviewed me. I was telling them how I moved here and how it was the biggest leap of faith. I said that I have applied to a lot of places, and I really just need someone to give me a chance. After the interview, I barely got down the road, and they wanted me to come in for a second interview with the front desk team. Here is where I started my journey with Novant Health. They hired me. It was a very busy office with 5 doctors. Everyone seemed really nice, especially the office manager. She and I got along really well. It's a couple weeks in and we are off for Christmas. It is our first holiday living away from home and being in a whole new place. My oldest son flew in from NY and we all went to my daughters' grandparents in Chapel Hill, NC. We had such a great time, as always with them. About six months in, I could see how some of my co-worker's true self started to come through. I was seeing some of the difference in the south from up north. The change started when my coworkers realized my children were biracial. I talked to my manager, and she spoke with them, but they are all set in their ways. I knew I could not be here much longer. My son was home by himself after school because I worked long hours, and didn't get home until after 6. It was hard, especially being in a new place. Me and my son went back to Pennsylvania for a quick trip to see my daughter graduate college. We had a party for her, and then we all headed back to Charlotte. I was so proud of her. She accomplished so much while in college. She was on the dean's list, started a dance team and just excelled.

At the new job now for a year, and I was like, I could not work in this anymore. I talked to my boss, and she said she knew about a new office opening and that I should apply. I talked to her district manager, and she wanted to meet with me about the position. We met up for an interview and it went really well. She said she had the perfect position for me. It was still with the same company, just another facility. It is a brand-new primary care office opening and she said I would be great. So, a little over a year and I was out of that office and into the new. I was so thankful to my boss at that time. God definitely had us in the same office for a reason. I had to get there to get here. In this first year, it was not all peaches and cream. I came to a place where I had no one, but I knew God said, "Go."

Having no one here is hard at times. I miss my friends, my son misses his, but we both know it is a process, so we keep pushing and trusting God. It is like walking around blind and you have no choice but to trust God to lead you. My son has met friends at the high school. They come to our apartment, and he goes to their homes. He is still having his anxiety attacks and I am trying to work through that as well. It is really bad. I took him to a doctor down here and just hoping that he can help him. I took my ex-husband for child support before we came, so when I moved, I let them know so they could update it. I had the order modified for review for my ex to help pay for our son's doctor office visits, especially since I am the one paying for his insurance. He contested it stating that our son does not have anxiety issues, which is so sad because he knew from when we went back home. So, instead of just helping your son, who is struggling with very bad anxiety, you contest it. Mind you, we have been here a year and you have yet to call him to see how he is doing, how is his new school, nothing. This is frustrating to me, but remember, he told our son he did not want anything to do with him when we were moving.

    We are at a new church, and it is different then what we are used to, worship is different, serving is different and I am not comfortable yet to put myself out there to serve or get connected like I normally would, but I will get there.

CHAPTER TWELVE
FIGURING OUT NEW

My daughter and I are going out to different places and events to hang out. She convinced me to get on a couple dating sites. We went back and forth about it, but she eventually convinced me. It was like dating on a thousand! I was going on dates day after day. It was actually fun, meeting different people and going to new places. I met a couple of really nice guys and was really just having a good time. Then I got another visitor from home! One of my friends came and once again it was so good to have some familiarity. We went to eat, hung out, went to church, went to a singles jazz event, and just had a really good time. About six months in, on the dating sites, I met a guy who after our first couple of dates said that he was interested in getting to know me more, and said he just wanted to date me, so we agreed.

We started seeing and talking to each other more. About three months of dating, he told me that he is married, but has been separated for 2 years. I instantly was pretty much triggered like, what, not again, not someone else. I remember telling him right away I was not going to continue this relationship and why wouldn't he have told me this, especially when I told him things that I had been through already. He said because he really liked me and did not want to scare me off. He said they were not together at all and would be divorced. I still said no, and he kept on trying. He was extremely persistent, sweet and convincing. And what did I do? Yes, I said OK. Did I not learn the last time? He worked a lot, but we still had our time together going out doing things and just hanging out. He knew the importance of who I date and them having a relationship with God, and going to church with me, is huge for me. He was going with me here and there, but not regularly.

    I remember, at the end of December my friend from home was coming for New Years. I was happy because I was in a space of not being sure of what to do in my relationship and I needed some time with my friend. I wanted him to finally be done with this divorce and stop procrastinating. Before she came, I was telling him how I felt again, and he reassured me that he was going to handle it. I ended up breaking up with him and said I just could not continue in it. My friend was with me for that New Years weekend. We made vision boards, talked, and just enjoyed our time together. Him and I had texted at this time and wished each other a happy new year. He texted me he missed me, and I said I missed him too.

A little after my friend left, he came over. I remember, it was early morning and we talked, and I cried, then fell asleep. Soon enough we got back together. So, we have been dating for almost a year and his job offered him a position in Florida. He said you can move in with me, and my son can start a new school. I knew I could not uproot him again, so now we are talking about a long-distance relationship, which I am really not into. He is saying we will be ok. He will be home on weekends, and he will fly me to see him as well. His lease was ending at his apartment, so he ended up moving into my apartment before he had to leave for Florida.

It was nice having him there, so we had more time together. He also helped me with the rent, which was extremely helpful. He is packed and ready to move. The alarm clock is set to get up early so we can pack the truck and drive to Florida for his move. That night, he gets a call from his district manager saying they want to keep him in Charlotte. I'm like, what! Yes God! He is meant to be here, and we are going to work this out. He had to travel to Florida some to start and then he will be only dealing with the Charlotte market. I am so excited about this. He was going back and forth for a short time. I went for a long weekend twice in the first month. I would relax at the pool while he was working, then we would go out to eat. It was nice having that time away together.

The one time I went we stayed at a resort, which was different. We had a good time. When he picked me up from the airport it was evening, and we were pulling into the resort. A number came up on his phone that I had noticed before that he said was his ex-girlfriend that he was dating before he met me. I asked why she was calling again, he said she is probably drinking again and that she will call at times when she is drunk. You already know that did not sit well with me and we started to argue. I was telling him he needed to answer it next time and tell her you are in a relationship. We have been together for a year now. I came back to Charlotte, then he came back as well. We planned to go back to Florida to see his family for his mom's birthday. It was my first time meeting everyone, so I was a little nervous. I got along so well with his sisters. They were really nice, and we really had a great time together. We exchanged numbers and stayed in touch.

As time goes on, we are back and forth in our relationship. He still didn't get his divorce, and that was really bothering me. "Why won't you just do it? I can clearly see you are not together so why hold onto it." He continued to say he was going to file for divorce. My lease was going to be up soon and after talking we decided we were going to get a bigger apartment together. As we were looking at places it made sense to us to just buy a house and get more for our money. I came across a house in a really nice development. We went to look at it and the person showing it ended up not being able to come. We drove through the development and saw the office was open, so we went in and talked to the lady. She was really nice and helpful. She showed us the model homes and said that some of the new builds were available to purchase. It was myself, my boyfriend and my daughter. The model was beautiful, it was big, and my daughter and I ran through it like we were little kids saying, "Look at this. OMG look at this!"

Then she said, "Yeah, this is my room."

We laughed. We went back to the office to talk to the women and got paperwork and went home to discuss it. Well, we did it. We bought a new house and were just so excited. He was now working in Charlotte only, so it was nice to have him home. He still did have to travel at times to different locations and to the corporate office every three months. Living in our house the kids are so happy to be in such a beautiful home. My son has started a new year in high school and his friends don't live far away, so they are at our house a lot. He is playing sports and keeping active, which helps at times with his anxiety attacks.

Now that we live together and are around each other a lot more than the first year of dating, you start to see things you did not see when you didn't live together. He is drinking at night after work, smoking cigarettes, and taking phone calls from different exes. The phone calls, he would say, are innocent and that they are just friends. The one ex who called when we were in Florida, I am seeing her still calling and texting. I'm like, uh yeah, I do not think she is still drinking and calling. Every time I would say something or argue, he would buy me something. I am like, "Do you want to be in this relationship?"

He would say, yes, he loves me and does not want anyone else. When he is traveling the calls to me are less or he is not answering when I call. He is telling me that it is because he is busy. I am busy as well with work. It is my son's sophomore year at school, and he is struggling in class and still having his anxiety attacks. One day, we were at home and my son wanted to call his dad, so he Facetimed him. I could hear him talking, telling him how he was doing in school and just about the area. I walked by and I said, "Hey, how are you?"

He said he was doing good, I said. "You should come down here and see him. He can show you around and hang out."

I said, "To save you money, you can stay here with us. We have a spare bedroom that you could stay in."

He laughed and said, "Nah, I'm not coming down there."

I thought he was just kidding, but he was serious. I honestly was being genuine. I was trying to be nice for our son's sake. This was the first time he had talked to his dad since we moved, almost 3 years ago. Part of me wanted to say you have traveled to see your other son through college and his football games, but it is ok my son is doing great here. But…I didn't. I kept my mouth closed and smiled and said, "OK, take care."

My daughter's friend from back home had moved to Charlotte almost a year ago. She started coming to our house. She started to stay over since she lived further out than we did, and it was closer to her job. Thanksgiving at our new house was really nice. My boyfriend's sister came, and his oldest daughter came. We all really had such a great time. It was nice to meet his daughter, who was so sweet. I enjoyed getting to know her, and to have his sister in our home was really nice. Christmas was just as nice. My oldest son came to visit from NY. We cooked brunch, laid around and had a good time.

Covid started kicking in. My daughter's friend ended up moving in and stayed in the one spare bedroom. It was nice having her there. She really became like family. She felt like another daughter to me. I love the relationship she and my daughter have. My relationship has been very on and off. One day he acts like he loves me and wants to be in it, and others nothing at all. I am trying to talk to him to see what is going on. Do you want to be in this or not? It is confusing me because he is on and off with what he is saying and showing me. I work in a doctor's office and Covid is in full force, so this has me on a thousand with stress. I am trying to keep my house super clean. I am not allowing any of the kids to go anywhere but work and home. I am cleaning like a crazy person. Making them get undressed in the garage, shoes off and getting groceries delivered. Yes, I was extremely extra.

We did have good times too. We would play games in the garage, play music, we did a sip and paint, and watched shows together. In time we were on each other's nerves. Well, I'm sure I was on their nerves more than they were on mine. They ended up going to see their friend a couple times. My son's anxiety is still going on and being in this house like this is not good for it, so that was an added stress. The girls ended up getting their own apartment a block away. I was so sad to see them go, but they still came over. They were literally around the corner. This was good for them to branch out on their own.

Well, it is my birthday and me and my daughter went to the outlets. After shopping, we went home, because my boyfriend was going to be cooking dinner for me. We pull up and go in the house and I'm like the kitchen is not lit up or smelling like food, he didn't cook! We walked in and I called his name and nothing. I turned the corner into the kitchen, and I heard, "Surprise!."

Three of my friends from home jumped out and surprised me. I was so shocked and surprised I screamed and ran over to them. My boyfriend popped out smiling. He was happy to see me happy. He knew how much I missed all of my friends from back home. It was such a great surprise. They told me that they had called my daughter and told her they were coming to surprise me for my birthday. Let me tell you, being in a new place by yourself year after year is hard.

My boyfriend started getting things ready and cooking a big dinner for us. We hung out in the kitchen talking and catching up with some wine and snacks. As my boyfriend is cooking, he pulled out a gift bag and reached his hand out to give it to me. I got up and walked over to get it from him. I opened the bag and took out the small box. I looked at him, and as I opened it up, he smiled and said, "Would you be my plus one?"

My mouth dropped open, my friends were like, "Wait what? What happened? Say it again." So, he asked me again and they started screaming and crying. We were all jumping around screaming. None of them knew, not even my daughter, he surprised all of us. My oldest son didn't even know. He was on his way driving from NY. He was moving to Charlotte because Covid was so out of control there. He walked in the door. What a surprise to him as well. When I say we had so much fun that night, whew yes, a night for the books! Me, my friends, my daughter, her friend from home, her friend from here, my sons, my boyfriend, my neighbor, my son's friend from NY. Listen to me! It was the best night ever! The next day we hung out, cooked, and had brunch. My friends bought matching pajamas for all of us, and we had a movie night. I did not want them to go back to PA, it was just an amazing weekend all the way around.

We had so many good times at our house. We would have cook outs, game nights, Sunday dinners, movie nights. It was just always a great time.

After everyone left, I was still so happy for an

amazing weekend, and I am engaged! Yes, I knew that he was still married but he finally went and filed for the divorce after a ton of conversations. I really want this relationship to work out. He is really a nice guy. He is caring, he will do anything for anyone, which is good and bad at the same time, because it can roll over into helping exes out. We were doing good though and talking about things. Church was still online, but we would watch together and talk about the sermon. He is telling me he loves me and wants to be with me, that there is no one else and wants no one else. Now, you know I want to believe him, but I need to really see it.

Covid still going on, so for Thanksgiving we had dinner outside in our driveway, and our neighbor set out his table in his driveway as well. We decorated our tables and everything. In our garage we had the food set up for everyone on tables. Music was playing. It was such a nice night.

Christmas, we had our brunch and after it my boyfriend was not himself. He gets like this from time to time, where he gets moody out of nowhere and then would disconnect from the family and the fun. I went and talked to him about it. Soon enough, he shook whatever it was off and came back to us.

So, for Christmas this year, my main gift was a puppy!!! Let me tell you, I have never had a dog and always said I did not want one. My youngest son and boyfriend brought it up one day, and at first, I was like, "No, absolutely not. I do not want a dog."

Then we started looking online. I was getting into looking. I saw the cutest puppies ever. They were Cockapoos. My son said, "Yes, mom, this kind of dog is good. They do not shed, and it is a hypoallergenic dog."

Well, me and my boyfriend one morning went to a breeder's house, and she brought out three puppies. I instantly fell in love with this tiny puppy that crawled over his siblings to get to me. He was the one. Teddy it is. They kept him until he had his shots and was ok to leave his mom. The end of December we went and picked him up and brought him home. All of my kids, plus my daughter's best friend, and another friend were there waiting with excitement. We all sat on the floor in a circle coaching him on as he went from one to the other. At this point, this is my new baby. He would cry early in the morning for us to take him out. Me and my boyfriend would get up to take him out and walk him. My boyfriend was working at home at this time because of Covid, so it really worked out great. He could take him out and take care of him. My son had online school as well, so he was able to help too. Teddy is such a good dog. He trained so fast. He didn't go to the bathroom in the house. In a time of craziness in the world, Teddy really brought some joy in all of our lives.

My relationship was very on and off, he is drinking a lot, smoking cigarettes and I am really trying to talk to him about it. It ends up in an argument every time. I don't care if after a long day of work you have a drink to wind down, but one led to another, to half a bottle, to being drunk and passing out. Some nights he would be up very late downstairs. I would end up just going to bed because it was just so late. He wasn't a mean drunk at all. He was actually extra nice, but it was not healthy for him or for our relationship. He is still talking to different exes. I am noticing now when he is drunk, and I am in bed, he is talking to that same ex that he was with before me. I am not acting like I don't see it. I call him on it, and he insists he is not. I ended up messaging the girl like, stop texting him. We are in a relationship, engaged and live together. She said, "Oh he didn't tell me that, so we are going to be friends."

I told him and he said again there is nothing. He is insisting that they don't talk at all. I explain again how his talking to his exes is going to be the thing that breaks us up. You cannot continue friendships with women and talking to them all the time. They call him for advice, ask questions, talk, early in the morning, all times of day and night. We are arguing a lot because I am like I cannot marry into something like this. It almost feels like I am in a competition with these women. I have talked to his sisters, and they try to talk to him as well, but he really is just not listening. He is busy with work and traveling. When he travels, I really don't hear from him. He normally says he is busy, or he falls asleep. In time, I find out when he travels, he is meeting women and seeing them.

One day, I was on FB, and noticed the same ex commenting on his posts. Yes, of course I clicked on her page, and then saw his comments on her things. I bring it up and still he is like it is nothing. She ends up posting a picture of herself with a guy on her page and this sets him off. I saw texts he is having with her asking her who he is, saying he still loves her, she says she still loves him, on and on and on. I'm like, what is going on? I brought it up to him, and at first, he was lying, then he said, "Yes, I still care about her."

I am like, "How can you ask me to marry you and now you're all over here?"

I was so sick. I went and slept in the spare room that night and he came in and got in the bed. I could not even be near him. A few days in, he said we are going to be ok, because he loves me. We talked and talked about it and said let's start over in dating. I would get an apartment and he would stay at the house and we would try it that way. I honestly felt numb and wasn't even sure what to do but knew I did need to go. So, I started actively looking for an apartment.

About a month in, I found one and would move in the following month. It is my son's senior year and I have just been so busy myself. He is running track and playing football. It has been just such a great year for him. I am so proud of him. Because of Covid, they did not get a prom, but they would have a graduation. He broke the school record for high jump and was just on fire. He was doing great in football. We were all at the games every Friday night. My boyfriend told me he had to travel to Atlanta, but he would be home for my son's senior night, the big game. Something in me was like, is he really going to travel for work, or was he going to meet her. He texted me when he landed, and we talked while he got off the plane. That was pretty much the last I heard from him. He would text and say he was busy at conferences or came in late and fell asleep. I called him and he did not answer.

I texted and said, do not forget it is my son's senior night and the importance of him being there for him. He was there in ways for my son, they had been building their own relationship in these couple years.

We get to the field and sit. We are packed deep for him tonight. I made collage posters of him to have out there. We all are so excited for this night and the game. The stadium is full, and we are ready. My boyfriend is not there yet. I go down to the field to get in line and stand with my son before we walk the field. At this point, I'm like if he comes, do not come down here with me. I texted my daughter, who was in the stands, and asked her if she wanted to walk the field with me for my son. She came down and asked him if he would like that, and he said yes. Now here he comes down towards the field. I'm looking at him like, I know you don't think at this point you are walking on the field with us. I was so mad he was so late. He came down and talked to my son and hugged him. I said you can go up in the stands with everyone else. I needed to be present for my son in this big moment.

    We walked onto that field, and yes, me and my daughter both cried. It has been a long road for my son to get to this point. He has worked so hard to be on this field. He had his ups and downs in the classroom, but he finally did it. He pushed past his anxiety, his fears, and having to deal with his dad never being there, especially in his journey of life in NC. He did it. I could not be any prouder or happier for him. Going back to the stands I felt the difference in my boyfriend's behavior. My daughter's friend said, "Oh wow, he is 'giving guilty of something' vibes over here." This game was so good, and my son was on fire. He was doing his thing out there. That week he got defensive player of the week. We all got home, and my son went out with his friends to celebrate. My boyfriend was bending over backwards being extra nice to me, so I was definitely thinking he was away with his ex, who he had been in contact with.

FIGURING OUT NEW

CHAPTER THIRTEEN
COURAGE

Five days later, I have the movers come and I am off to my new apartment. I have very mixed emotions going on. Two of my friends from home came to my new apartment on my moving day. As I am moving in, I am noticing this apartment is an absolute mess. I couldn't stop the movers, because they are on the clock, so they are flying in and out putting my items in the apartment. My friends come walking in and I instantly start to cry hugging them. I am emotional because my relationship is half in, half out. The apartment clearly was not walked by the complex, because so much is wrong up there. When I found this place, it was so nice out front. The office was beautiful, along with all the amenities.

When I toured, I was taken into a model, because the apartment I was getting was not ready yet. The model was so beautiful it made me feel a little better about moving from our new home. I asked her if the apartment I am going to move into is just like this and will it be cleaned and ready? She said, "Yes, absolutely."

So, here I am, all moved in. My friends are here to help me set up, and to support me. The apartment is disgusting, and they agreed. My one friend is only here for that day. She had to go right back. I so appreciated her even coming with her being so busy. That meant so much to me. It meant a lot that they both came to support me. We immediately started going through the house room by room looking at everything and taking pictures. They are like, "Nette, you cannot stay here. This is so bad."

The front door key barely worked, and the door and frame looked like someone busted into it over and over. We all walked down to the office to talk to them. As we are walking to the office, we see the trash area and the dumpster is overflowing all over the place, so that is a whole other thing. The leasing consultant said the manager was not there. I explained to them all of the issues and showed them pictures. At first, she had an attitude, but realized, oh yeah, this is a lot. They said there were no other units available, but they could put work orders in for everything. "Are you kidding me? Do you know how long that will take?"

She said, "Yes, it will take a while for everything to be done, but it will get done."

I talked with my friends, and we all agreed this place was a hard NO. I called my boyfriend and told him what was going on. He said just come back home. Let them know you want out of the lease and move back. I went back to the office and said, "I want out of this lease. This is unacceptable and unfit living conditions."

I said, "Whoever walked this unit could not possibly think this is the way someone should live."

I said, "Clearly, no one walked this unit."

She said she would speak to the manager. I told them I need maintenance to come right away so we can lock the door, since all of my belongings are in there. When I say that was a whole other long, drawn-out issue. I had to go back and forth to the office to get someone to come. We waited for over an hour for this apartment complex maintenance man to come. He finally came and said he fixed it but did not. He had to go get another lock. As he is talking, he said, he never even came to change the lock when the other person moved out. I'm like what in the world is going on here. Yes, it is time to go. So, I pack some things up, to go back to the house.

I called the movers to see if they could come back to move everything back. They were done for the day but gave me a date they could do it a couple days later. We all went back to the house and showered, talked, and hung out. My one friend had to leave in the morning and my other friend stayed with me. Her daughters were with her as well, but they went to my daughter's apartment. I was so overwhelmed and exhausted. It took me so long to find this apartment, so now I'm like Lord, please help me find something else. The next day the movers brought everything back to the house and we had them put everything back in all the rooms. Oh, my goodness, it was all just so exhausting, but we got it all done. I was going to be staying in the spare bedroom while I was there. I was so glad my friend decided she was going to stay with me for a few days. We would cook and have Easter together. All the kids, and us would be together. The day before Easter we all decided to go out in the afternoon. Me, my friend from home, her daughters, my daughter, and her best friend. We went uptown and had a couple drinks and appetizers. We laughed a whole lot and man I needed it. The girls all went back to Jada's and me and my friend went to the house. We started prepping and cooking for Easter dinner. My boyfriend got back to the house at the same time as us. We were all cooking and listening to music. He said he had to go outside to get something, and we continued cooking, talking, and laughing. I realized he had been gone for a while now, so I went out the front door and saw his car in the driveway. I could hear talking through the car speakers.

I could hear a female talking. So, I walked over to the driver side thinking he would roll down the window, but he didn't. He locked the door. I'm like, hold up. Why are you locking the door and not opening up? I knocked on his window and said, "Open the door."

He ignored me. I said it again. He cracked the door and I said, "Who are you talking to?" He did not respond, but just looked up at me. I said, "No seriously, who is on the phone?"

Again, he said nothing. I said, "Clearly you are on the phone with a female. I heard her."

I said, "You don't have to be quiet now because I am standing here."

I said the girl's name, his ex, who it probably was. I said, "I'm sure it is you."

"She answered and said, "Yes."

I looked at him like wow, surprised but yet, not. I said, "I have been gone a couple days and you are still doing this. You just said you wanted for us to work things out."

Again, he did not say a thing. He just looked at me with a blank look. So, now she says, "Yes, we have been talking."

She said, "I was away with him in Atlanta." I said, "Yeah, I figured that was the case. He told me he was going there for work."

She said, "Yeah, no. He was with me, and we were intimate."

They had met up other times as well. I looked at him in disgust and I went into the house. I was so angry, I started to cry telling my friend what happened. He said that he was going to a hotel and would be back tomorrow. After he left, my son came home. I was on the couch laying down. My friend told him what was going on. He just came and sat by me, hugged me, and asked if I was ok.

The next day was Easter, and everyone came over. He texted me and said, "I am so sorry I ruined everything."

I didn't hear back from him that day. When he came home, we talked. I decided I was going to stay here. At this point, it is what it is. I will stay in the spare bedroom, and I am not going to help with any of the bills. I am going to save so I will have money for rent when the time comes. My son needs to finish up high school with no more interruptions, so this is it until after he graduates. We had all of April to August. It was uncomfortable at first, but I had to get the mindset of this is it for now, and you will be ok.

At this time, my son is still in school, and I am going to his track meets and my ex is coming to see him as well. I didn't have a problem with that because

I knew my son wanted him there and needed that male support. Trust me, at first, I was really hurt and messed up from this, but I had to get the mindset that it didn't work and that's ok. As for my son, I knew it was hard on him. He said that my ex was the closest thing he ever had to a dad. So, I was ok with the relationship that they still had. That was between them.

My time here in the house was definitely different than the norm, but we were civil to each other. He ended up helping me pay off my credit cards and I was able to save some money. My daughter and her best friend moved to another area in Charlotte. Her best friend started working at the church, so they were going to that location. My daughter's best friend was like, "Ok Miss Annette, it is time to jump back in. You have been away long enough. You've been watching it on tv, and it is time to come back."

She said, "You need to start serving, you know that is who you are. So cut it out and come to the University City location."

I said, "Ok", and started to go, then started to serve. It was different because I didn't know anyone yet, but this location felt more like home. I found an apartment complex to move into. It was a new complex, and in a nice area right by my job. It was a little high, but I figured I am saving so I can use that towards my rent every month.

My son is at the end of his senior year, and I cannot believe it. I decorated the house for him so when he came home after practice he would be surprised. The next day will be graduation.

He did it! Graduation day is here, and I am beyond proud. It has been the longest journey, but he did it. He pressed through every struggle and his anxiety. Him being involved in sports really did help him. Me, my daughter, and my son's girlfriend went to his graduation. My ex came and met us there and this meant everything to my son. No, his dad did not go to his graduation, his senior night or anything else. No, he didn't call him. Nothing. As soon as graduation was over, we went straight to his track meet, he was still jumping and still killing them out there.

A month later he is off to college, I am so happy for him, so proud of him and of course, I am an emotional mess. He is my youngest and last to go. I will be an empty nester, which I am not excited about. He said, "Mom, I will be ok, and you will be too. You have Teddy."

After my son graduated, me and my ex decided to sell our home. With saving in this time and my credit cards being paid off, I am in a position to buy a home. The housing market is crazy at this time though. People are selling houses in a day and there are lines of people to just look at one house. I put in offers on two different homes, but my offers were not accepted. I was down to two weeks before moving into the apartment. My realtor called me and said, there was an open house and did I want to go. He said it was about to end so I would need to hurry and go right away. I asked my ex if he could go with me to look at it, since my realtor couldn't make it in time. So, we went over and walked through. There was not one person there. It was in an area that was still close to my job. It was a two-bedroom townhouse. I wanted three, but I was open to it. It was older and needed some work done inside. My ex said that it was still in good shape. He said he had people he would have come to do the cosmetic things for me. I called my realtor and said he could put my offer in. They accepted my offer. I was so happy and so excited. It was literally the last minute before I would have had to move into the apartment. I knew this was all God. My ex called his people and they moved quickly. They went in and painted the whole house inside. All new floors, new bathroom, new kitchen cabinets and counter. I was so happy to be able to get this all done before moving in. Well, most of it, some of it I had to live through them working in it. I was still staying at the house with my ex until it sold, then I moved into my place. It was definitely different moving into my house by myself, but I was so thankful.

I was getting more involved in church. My word for the new year was Courage. Courage to stand on my own. Courage to let go and to choose me. So, I got a call from my daughter's best friend, and she said, "Miss Annette, how about leading an Egroup?"

Instantly I said, "Oh no. I am not leading an Egroup, but I am in one."

She is pushing me, "C'mon this is so you. You would be great."

She said, "I already know what you would be great at, but you tell me what type of group you would like to lead, if you could do it."

I said, "I would lead a group for single moms."

She said, "Yes! Yes, you would be great."

She said, "I am putting you on the list." I said, "No. I am not doing it." She pushed, and still put me on the list.

About a month later, it is time to start. I am so nervous. Remember, my word is courage, so now I am praying for God to give me the courage to lead the Egroup. I read the material and wrote out my notes so that I was prepared for our first night. We would meet once a week after work at the church. I remember, the first night when everyone came in and sat down. I said,

"I'm letting you all know this is my first time leading an Egroup and I am really nervous."

Everyone was so nice. It was a great group of women. The next week was even better, as I shared my story, then other women started to open up. To some, this may be so small, but for me this was so big. I did it! Courage. God really gave me the courage to do it.

My ex and I continued to be friends and he would ask me if I wanted to work things out again. Part of me wanted to and the other part said, no, don't be crazy. I knew I had to move on for myself. We never dated again although he asked me at different times in the next year about getting back together. I actually considered it. I did. I knew he was handsome. I knew he was a nice guy. I knew he was a hard worker. I knew he was a provider. Yes, I could have a nice big house, vacations, I wouldn't struggle, I would go on nice dates and anything that I wanted, but I wouldn't be happy. I didn't like all of the drinking. I would wonder who he was with when he traveled, which ex is he still talking to. As women, we will stay in something to not struggle, to have all of the nice things. But all of that cannot make you happy. You will be empty inside.

Although we no longer were dating, he knew I was struggling financially and offered to still help me with my car payment and gas for over a year. In the beginning of him helping me I was like, yes you should help me. You flipped my whole life upside down. But as time went on I almost felt bad. I have never, ever, just taken money for help. I have never been that woman. I have always had way too much pride to ask for anything. I would struggle before asking for help. But this time he offered, and I took it. Did I need it? Yes. There was not enough money to pay the bills, but I knew I had to stop. I didn't even see him. He would just Zelle it to me. He was doing it to be kind. Doing it so I would not struggle, but God was telling me to stop. I would say, "Ok God, next month I will stop."

I would say the same thing every month. Everything in Charlotte is just going up and up. It is so expensive to live here. I was applying to so many jobs to try and make more money so I could stop taking it. I started working a part time job to stay afloat. I had to take care of my son in college as well, so the second job would take care of his food, his gas, haircuts and whatever else he needed. It was exhausting though. I would drive almost an hour to my full-time job, and then back home to run in the house, change and go straight to my second job. One day, I called my daughter's best friend to talk. We have a good relationship. We called each other at times when I needed to talk. She has become literally like a daughter to me. I remember calling her and I just started crying.

I was overwhelmed with struggling financially, struggling with the difference of living in the south than the north, the segregation of it. I was thinking about moving out of the area, but definitely not moving back home. Feeling alone, not lonely, but alone. There is a difference. At this time, I had been down here over five years, and yes, I have met people. I have gone out and done things, but there was no real closeness in friendships. I was serving. I was pouring into others, including all of my kids. I knew God was using me in many ways, but that didn't take away the tiredness or emptiness. She said, "Miss Annette, first you have to stop taking the money from him. I know it is hard, but how is God going to bless you if you are still taking it?"

Mind you, God had been speaking to me for a while about this, but I ignored it. I was trying to rationalize it with her saying, "I'm not sleeping with him or anything. He is just helping me."

She again said, "Miss Annette, how is God going to bless you if you are depending on this man?"

We talked about how things are different down here like segregation and she understood that as well. I talked about how I am working like a crazy person, serving at church, pouring into people at church, pouring into people at work, pouring into my kids, including her. They will all call me, and I drop everything to talk, to listen, to encourage. I am checking in on everyone, but no one is checking in on me. I felt I was doing all this, and I was running on fumes. I was literally empty. We agreed I needed to take some time to fast and pray and see what God is saying. She sent me a sermon from church that our pastor's wife had preached titled, *"Running On Empty."*

I remember, I had seen her preach this at church, but I was like, ok, let me go back and watch it again. Let me tell you, this thing was literally everything I had said to her in our conversation. She started to say, "You are empty from running around, working, being there for everyone, supporting others and your emptiness reminds you of your loneliness. Do you ever feel the weight of others needing you? You feel like you keep going and have nothing left. You're at the end of yourself. The same routine, you wake up, go to work, come home, and cook, clean, and go to bed. You feel almost empty and no real joy. But God does some of His best work when you feel empty. When you are feeling empty, cry out to God."

I'm listening to her preaching and listening for God. I'm like, God, I hear you. Don't pretend to yourself that you are ok. It is ok to be in a space of not being ok. Recognize it and talk to God about it.

You are doing everything to fill that emptiness. You are carrying everything on your shoulders. Being busy does not replace emptiness. It may mask it for a little, but it does not replace it. And because you are just masking it, you start to believe that no one cares, and you feel empty and alone. We look to find comfort in people and in things, but you really can't find it in them. Only God can fill those empty feelings and moments. Cry out to Him. He is waiting for you to call on Him. He hears your silent cries. He hears when you have no words at all. What we do is we either hold it all in until we can't anymore, or we call everyone to talk. We have to stop calling on God last. Just talk to Him. It is really just having a conversation. The enemy does not want you to call on God. He wants you to think you have nothing. That you don't have anyone and are just alone. He said to keep pouring out. His strength will come as you pour. It will feel like a sacrifice, but He will sustain you. I am continuing to fast, pray and I am writing. I am writing not even realizing I am about to write my book.

    The next day, I watched another sermon, this was from our pastor. I have seen this sermon in church as well, but this is one I came to, so I am watching. The sermon title is, *"Enough Until It Comes."*

    As soon as he said the title, I'm like, oh yeah.

Here we go. One of the first things he said was, that "God promised to give you enough until it comes."

Then he asked, "How good are you at letting God meet your needs? In times of need, will you run to God or someone else?"

I'm like, ok, you are starting out from the jump talking to me. He said, "Everything you depend on that does not come from God will dry up, if you depend on them to meet the needs God is designed to meet. Remember the times when you didn't have, but God kept you and provided for you. It didn't even make sense."

When he said that it took me back to so many times in my life when I didn't have, and God provided. And at times in my life there was physically not enough money to pay the bills, but the bills were paid every month. He will meet your needs differently in different seasons on purpose. He didn't forget you or leave you. He is moving you, new patterns, and new things. God was definitely speaking clearly to me in this time of fasting and praying. Both sermons were originally preached a year apart from each other and they both tied in together. It was definitely not a coincidence. It was definitely for me. God spoke so clearly in so many ways, I wrote, and wrote, and wrote. The one thing God spoke to me over and over was, "Nothing will be enough, until I am enough."

I knew what this meant, and I knew what I had to do. For the first time in over a year I paid my first car payment and gas. Gas for me was so high because of my commute to work, and my car payment was high. Although God made it clear, I was not to take any more money. It does not mean it was easy to do. I am human and I worried and stressed about making ends meet. I was watching God move though. My team at church was growing and I was connecting more with some of the women and becoming friends. New friends may not look like what you had before. That does not mean it's not good. It is just different. It is a different time, a different season. I am realizing now, that everywhere that I am, God has placed people there for me to minister to. My full-time job, my part time job, my church, there has been person after person I have encouraged, prayed with and walked through things with. We plant the seeds and God does the rest. Everything I have done and been through, I would have never thought that God would be using me.

I have been working two jobs for a year now and I am exhausted and burned out. I know I need to work both jobs to stay afloat, but I got to a point where I said, I cannot do this anymore. I said, "God I know on paper I have to work this second job right, but I am telling You I mentally and physically cannot do one more day working this second job."

I started to cry and said, "I can't. I just can't anymore," and I quit.

I said, "God I am putting every bit of faith in You, trusting that You will make a way. Instead of nights at work I am going to spend my nights writing my book. I am finally going to do it. You told me many years ago to write, so that is what I am going to do."

The young teenage girl I introduced you to in the beginning, has grown to be a 55 year-old woman. She is still learning. She is still growing. She is forgiven and has forgiven. She is still seeking God in everything she does. Although I feel that I was stripped of so many things as a teenager, it ultimately made me who I am. I have so many scars, but they are beautiful, and they are me. I made the decision while writing this book that when I am done, I will be getting into some counseling to just talk these things out. The things I have held onto subconsciously all of these years, not even realizing the pattern and cycle that it all created. I was taking my hurts and brokenness into every new relationship, just wanting to be loved. I never dealt with any of it. I never healed. I just carried it all like heavy luggage.

I felt I was giving the love over and over and not being loved back. I was just accepting whatever was being given to me. I knew I deserved better, and I wanted better, but instead I stayed and created more brokenness for me to carry. I never chose me. We all want and deserve to be loved, and it will come. Just wait on it and do not settle. I don't know how I did it all the years when I did not know God, but I am forever thankful that He knew me from the very beginning. That He loved me so much, that He kept His hand on me, even through all the years of my bad decisions. His grace and mercy are like nothing I could have ever imagined. He has hid me. He has protected me. He has provided for me, and He has kept me through it all.

COURAGE

CHAPTER FOURTEEN
RESURFACE

This year, I had two words that God gave me, Healing and Resurface. Sometimes, when He gives you a word, a physical word, a scripture, or even a season in your life, you don't even realize what any of it even means for you. Pay attention to every word, every season, and write it down. It is for a reason, and little by little, it will speak to you.

A few months before the new year, I was in bed, and I was praying, crying, and pretty much begging God to please speak to me. I was tired, overwhelmed, and just trying to figure out what I need to be doing. I went to sleep, and that same night, I heard one word. He gave me a single word. I jumped up, grabbed my phone, and wrote it down. It was very clear, but I had no clue what it meant. The word was, "Resurface."

I sat up trying to figure out what in the world could this mean. I opened the bible app to see if there was a certain scripture, or message, and I came up with nothing. I went back to sleep. The next day, I started again to try and figure it out. I looked up the definitions just trying to see what God was trying to tell me. It said, "Putting on a new coat. To renew, to come back up to the surface."

Still, not sure what it means for my life. So, when the new year came, and we had to write our words down, God gave me another word, "Healing." So, I wrote them both down. I kept listening to see what God was saying, and what He was going to do. I can tell you exactly what they both mean now. I am at the end of my book, and it all ties in. The healing is not just for me, but for my children, and for you. We stop all the hurts and brokenness here. We break the generational curses from repeating themselves right here, right now. We will resurface and come up as new from this book. I pray this book stirs up something new in you. Be confident in yourself. Love yourself. Choose you. Be healed and walk in your newness. Come up new!

REFLECTION

I wanted to take a minute to speak to the single moms. I know it isn't easy, doing everything by yourself. It is the most exhausting, yet most rewarding thing you could ever do. Know that God is right there with you. He sees you and hears every cry. He is catching each tear and turning them into blessings for you and your children. He loves you and has created you differently. He has given you a strength like no other. Keep pushing. Keep trusting Him.

ABOUT THE AUTHOR

Annette Orchulli's journey from her hometown of Easton, Pennsylvania to her current residence in Charlotte, North Carolina has been marked by a tapestry of experiences that have shaped her into the remarkable woman she is today. Her life is rich with love, resilience, and an unwavering commitment to family.

As a Clerical Supervisor at a pediatric doctor's office, Annette dedicates her professional life to ensuring the well-being of young patients. Her role reflects her genuine passion for helping others, a trait that extends far beyond her workplace.

Annette is a proud mother of three wonderful grown children - Christopher, Jada, and Josiah. Her children are not just her pride and joy; they are her everything, a source of inspiration, and a driving force in her life. She cherishes every moment spent with them and her dear friends, as these connections are her true treasures.

Annette's experiences have cultivated in her a profound empathy for young people, women, and single mothers. Her heart is dedicated to uplifting and supporting these individuals, offering them the strength and encouragement they need to navigate life's challenges.

With her book, "Protected: A Journey of Resilience and Renewal," Annette Orchulli aspires to be a beacon of hope and transformation. Through her own experiences, she hopes to inspire others and make a lasting impact on their lives. Annette's story is a testament to the power of love, resilience, and the unwavering desire to help those in need, making her book a potential catalyst for change in the lives of her readers.

Annette Orchull

Music For Your Soul